HOW TO MAKE
SOURDOUGH

HOW TO MAKE
SOURDOUGH

45 recipes for great-tasting sourdough breads that are good for you, too.

EMMANUEL HADJIANDREOU

photography by Steve Painter

RYLAND PETERS & SMALL
LONDON • NEW YORK

Design, Photographic Art Direction and Prop Styling Steve Painter
Commissioning Editor Nathan Joyce
Production Controller David Hearn
Editorial Director Julia Charles
Art Director Leslie Harrington
Publisher Cindy Richards

Indexer Ingrid Lock

First published in 2016
by Ryland Peters & Small
20–21 Jockey's Fields
London WC1R 4BW
and
1452 Davis Bugg Road
Warrenton, NC 27589
www.rylandpeters.com

20 19 18 17 16 15 14 13 12 11

Text © Emmanuel Hadjiandreou 2016
Design and photographs
© Ryland Peters & Small 2016

ISBN 978 1 84975 704 1

A catalogue record for this book is available from the British Library.

A cataloging-in-progress record is available from the Library of Congress.

Printed and bound in China

Notes

• All spoon measurements are level, unless otherwise specified.
• Ovens should be preheated to the specified temperature. Recipes in this book were tested using a fan/convection oven. If using a regular oven, follow the manufacturer's instructions for adjusting temperatures.
• All eggs are UK medium/US large unless otherwise specified. Recipes containing raw or partially cooked egg should not be served to the very young, very old, anyone with a compromised immune system or pregnant women.

contents

Introduction

I would like to thank everyone who has supported and purchased *How to Make Bread* and *Making Bread Together*. I love to hear that people are making bread from both books and that they're having so much fun making it.

In this book, I am introducing you to sourdough and long fermentation. I want to show you that the most important ingredient is time and waiting for things to develop. Also that you really do not need lots of sourdough to make a great loaf of bread.

Some of the recipes I have turned from yeasted dough into a sourdough. I find that once you understand how all the ingredients work, you can make a great product. Bread will always differ from season to season because of the weather and the new-season flour, to name but a couple of things. Some of the ingredients will be a bit more challenging than others so have patience and take it one step at a time. It's really important to read the recipe thoroughly, make sure you weigh out all your ingredients, dry and wet, and that you can see all your ingredients before you start mixing. You'll also achieve the best results with good-quality ingredients.

Throughout my baking career, I have introduced bread making to lots of people and it is so pleasing to hear that they are enjoying making great bread. I never get tired of making a loaf of bread because the magic starts from the time you start mixing and continues through to the moment you take the loaf out of the oven.

I hope you will have as much fun creating all the breads in this book as I have really enjoyed putting the recipes together. Lastly, do remember that if your sourdough is not bubbling, your bread will not rise.

Happy baking!

Tools, equipment and tips

Accuracy is crucial in bread making. For this reason, I have given all ingredients in metric weights first (including salt, yeast and liquids), followed by American cups and/or ounces, teaspoons or tablespoons. I highly recommend that you weigh everything on high-precision electronic scales, but of course it's up to you. A properly measured cup of white flour weighs 120 g or 4¼ oz. When measuring flour by the cup, spoon it into the measuring cup and scrape off the excess.

Precision electronic scales: If you choose to weigh your bread-making ingredients (rather than measure them in cups and spoons), you want scales that can weigh between 1 g and about 3 kg. They tend to come in 1-g, 2-g or 5-g graduations, so make sure you buy scales with a 1-g graduation for the most accurate measurement of ingredients like salt and water.

At least 1 large mixing bowl (approximately 2-litre/8-cup capacity) and at least 1 small mixing bowl (approximately 1-litre/4-cup capacity): You want to be able to fit one bowl on top of the other snugly. You can either upturn the smaller one and put it inside the bigger bowl; or you can upturn the larger one and place it over the smaller one. I find this the most convenient way to mix wet and dry ingredients, as well as providing an easy covering while the dough rises. I normally use a plastic or Pyrex bowl, but if you use Pyrex, make sure you rinse the bowl in warm water to warm it up if it has been stored in a cold cupboard.

Deep roasting tray: You will need to put a cup of water in this to create steam in your oven. Put the pan on the bottom of the oven before preheating it.

Loaf pans: 500-g/6 x 4-inch (or 1-lb.) and 900-g/8½ x 4½-inch (or 2-lb.) capacities are what we mainly use in this book.

Proofing/dough-rising baskets: These come in various shapes and sizes and are used to hold dough during proofing. They shape the dough and create attractive patterns on the crust of the baked bread. They are made from a variety of materials. These baskets are not essential to bread making but are a good investment for the avid baker.

Proofing/baker's linen (couche) or clean tea/kitchen towel: This is a thick linen traditionally used to support dough inside a proofing/dough-rising basket (especially French baguettes) and also to absorb a little moisture from the dough, which helps to form the bread crust. You can also use thick, heavy, clean tea/dish cloths for this and to cover dough during proofing.

Baking stone: Avid bakers might like to invest in a baking stone. Baking stones come in a variety of materials and thicknesses, and are designed to help bake bread evenly. They should be put in the oven and preheated slowly at the same time as the oven. If you put a cold stone in a very hot oven, it can crack. Alternatively, preheat a heavy baking sheet flipped upside-down for 30–45 minutes.

Bread or pizza peel: Used to slide bread into the hot oven.

Baking sheets: You will often need more than one baking sheet if you are making individual pastries or similar. For pastries, bake from cold on a sheet lined with silicon-coated paper in a preheated oven (not on a baking stone).

Metal dough scraper or sharp, serrated knife: A metal dough scraper makes dividing dough accurate and easy, but a sharp serrated knife works well, too.

Plastic dough scraper: This scrapes dough and stray ingredients cleanly from the edge of a mixing bowl so that all the ingredients are well incorporated.

Lamé: This is a small, very sharp blade like a scalpel to score and slash the surface of the bread before baking. You can use a clean razor blade securely attached to the end of a wooden coffee stirrer or a small, very sharp knife instead.

As well as the more specialist pieces of equipment above, you will also need many of these common kitchen items:

Baking parchment or silicon-coated paper
Fine sieve/strainer or flour sifter
Kitchen thermometer
Measuring jug/pitcher or cups and spoons
Pastry brush
Rolling pin
Round cake pans
Shower cap or a clean plastic bag
Wire rack for cooling
Wooden spoon

Sourdough: the crucial components

Sourdough bread is wonderfully easy to make. It all begins with two ingredients: flour and water. Flour contains two magic ingredients, though: wild yeast spores and lactic acid bacteria. Mixing flour and water starts the fermentation process, during which the wild yeast spores multiply and release carbon dioxide. This mixture, called a starter (see pages 16–17), is what bakers used for centuries before packaged yeast was invented.

Flour

Flour is the starting point for bread and can be made from many different grains. The majority of the flour used in this book is wheat flour. Each grain of wheat contains three main elements: bran, endosperm and germ. The way in which the wheat is milled determines which parts of the grain remain in the flour, and which are lost. There are two ways of making flour from wheat: stone-grinding and roller-milling. Stone-ground flour crushes grains between two stones, whereas roller-milling crushes grains through a series of metal rollers and sieves. Stone-ground flour is healthier as it retains all the natural vitamins and oils in the grain. This is because everything that goes in one side comes out the other side, and nothing is lost or thrown away. Roller-milling, by contrast, sifts out the bran and germ. The strip of images to the left shows wheat in various forms: (A) entire wheat kernels, also called wheat berries; (B) chopped wheat; (C) milled wheat (similar

to the texture of semolina); (D) wholemeal/wholewheat flour; and (E) stone-ground white flour. The images above show a mini stone mill in action.

Water

Water brings all the ingredients together and activates the wild yeast, which is responsible for making the bread rise. When water is combined with the flour, the proteins gluten and gliadin start to form, which is what makes dough elastic and easy to shape. The water also brings out the starch, which is the food source for the yeast. You need to be careful with the temperature of the water you use when it comes to sourdough or barm. Really cold water will slow the yeast down, while heat will kill it. A hand-warm temperature (between 30–37°C/86–99°F) is ideal. Make sure you can drink the water you use to make your bread. If you can't drink it, the sourdough or barm will not like it. If this is the case, use bottled water.

Wild yeast

Spores of wild yeast exist in flour. Mixing flour and water gives the yeast an environment in which to multiply. Lactobacilli (see right) eats up the carbohydrates in the flour, breaking it down into simple sugars. These simple sugars are a food source for the wild yeast, which releases bubbles of carbon dioxide. It is this fermentation process that makes the bread rise.

Gluten

Gluten is the web that traps the carbon dioxide that the yeast produces, and in many ways, it's similar to bubble gum. When you chew gum, it starts off hard, and if you try to blow bubbles then, the gum will break. Once you've chewed the gum for a while, the gum becomes nice and elastic and you will be able to blow bubbles. Similarly, the more you knead dough, the more elastic it becomes. Once the gluten is developed, it can trap lots of carbon dioxide, which makes the bread rise.

Lactic acid and acetic acid

Wild yeast (sourdough) naturally contains lactobacilli, a type of lactic acid bacteria that develops when flour and water are mixed together and start to ferment. Lactic acid and acetic acid break down the gluten, making it easier to digest. It is the lactobacilli that gives sourdough its distinctive sour taste. It also helps sourdough bread to keep for longer than other loaves.

Salt

Salt is also really important in the bread-making process. Not only does it season the bread, adding flavour, but it also reacts with the protein in the flour to strengthen the gluten and make it more elastic. Salt also helps to give the crust a lovely colour when the loaf is baking. It is also a preservative, helping to prolong the bread's shelf life. However, bear in mind that too much salt can prevent the bread from rising.

Ancient grains

The increasingly popular term 'ancient grains' refers to whole grains that are largely unchanged over the last few centuries. It would have been one of these grains, most likely einkorn or emmer, that was used to make the first loaf of bread, and this first loaf would have most likely been a version of the sourdough bread that we know and love today. The category 'ancient grains' distinguishes the grains that have been cultivated since the beginnings of time from the grains that have been selectively bred and altered over the last few centuries. Modern wheat has been selectively cultivated and is often heavily refined. It is the descendant of three ancient strains of wheat – spelt, einkorn and emmer. By contrast, ancient grains are considered to be more natural and healthier, bringing us more vitamins, minerals, fibre and protein than modern wheat. Ancient grains are wonderful additions to bread. With the exception of the gluten-free grains, ancient grains contain different amounts of gluten, so it's advisable to mix them into wheat flour in certain proportions. The following is a list of the ancient grains used in this book.

Barley: Barley is one of the oldest cultivated grains and one of the hardiest. It contains the most fibre out of all the whole grains. Unusually, the fibre is found throughout the whole grain rather than just in the outer bran layer. It is also high in antioxidants, vitamins and minerals.

Buckwheat: Slightly surprisingly, buckwheat is not related to wheat at all. It isn't even a grass, but rather a relation of rhubarb and sorrel that is cultivated for its grain-like seeds. Buckwheat is gluten-free and is a popular substitute for wheat. It contains the important antioxidant rutin, which helps to prevent against heart disease.

Einkorn: Einkorn is widely considered to be the oldest precursor to wheat, and was first cultivated around 12,000 years ago. It has very small, rice-like, chewy kernels that have a distinctive nutty flavour. In Italy, it's known as 'farro piccolo'.

Emmer: Emmer is another ancient relation of wheat and is great for making pasta, much like its younger relative durum wheat. It is known as 'farro' in Italy. Emmer is high in protein and low in gluten, and is therefore a popular option for people with wheat sensitivity. It has a richer, deeper flavour than spelt.

Kamut: Kamut is in fact a trademarked name for a specific variety of Khorasan wheat, and derives from an ancient Egyptian word for wheat. It is a particularly large grain – roughly double the size of modern wheat – and is prized for its nutty flavour. It contains higher levels of protein than modern wheat, as well as more vitamin E.

Spelt: One of the oldest cultivated crops, spelt is a variety of wheat and can be used instead of modern wheat for many recipes. It contains more protein than modern wheat, and despite falling out of favour as a crop from the Middle Ages onwards, it has recently become popular as a health food.

Teff: Teff is a type of grass that yields a very small grain. It is native to Ethiopia and Eritrea, where it is used to make a flatbread called *injera*. It is gluten-free and high in protein and calcium. It is prized for its flavour but suffers from low yield compared with wheat.

Quinoa: Quinoa is a small, light-coloured round grain and it originally heralds from the Andes, where it was cultivated by the Inca people. Like buckwheat, it is not a true grain, being a relation of Swiss chard and beets. It is prized as a complete protein, meaning that it contains all of the amino acids that our bodies are not able to make on their own.

A selection of grains and flour
Clockwise from top left: einkorn, barley, teff, buckwheat, quinoa, spelt, kamut and emmer.

GETTING STARTED

How to make a sourdough starter

For generations, bakers used to keep a pot of live culture made of a flour and water mixture, and 'fed' it daily or weekly to keep it alive and active. Today, this is known as a sourdough starter. Making your own sourdough starter is very easy. It takes 5 days to make a fully active sourdough 'starter' and you can use all kinds of flour to make it. It also requires feeding to keep it going. Once the starter is bubbling, it can be built up and used the next day to make bread. Keep the starter in the fridge when you are not using it.

Just two ingredients

You'll first need a container that can be sealed, like a clean miniature jam jar. Alternatively, you can use a larger jar like a kilner jar, but remove the rubber seal so a little more air will get into the jar. To create your own sourdough starter, mix 1 teaspoon of flour and 1–2 teaspoons of water (depending on the type of flour you use) to get a batter consistency. As for the type of flour, you can use most types to make sourdough. All of the sourdough starters you will need for this book (with the exception of the beer barm starters used in the Cultured Sourdoughs chapter) can be created using the instructions on the opposite page. I wouldn't use bleached flour as all the natural goodness (in my opinion) has been taken out. Avoid self-raising/rising flour and corn and potato starch too. I tend to use organic flour because it doesn't contain any chemicals that will affect or even kill the sourdough. As for the water, I always say if you can't drink the water, then neither should the sourdough! So to be on the safe side, start with bottled water. I also use hand-warm water, as cold water will slow it down. Ideally, you're looking for a temperature of between 30–37°C (86–99°F).

Use your nose

Make sure you smell your mixture often, as it will change during the fermentation process. You will notice a big difference by Day 3 and the batter should start to bubble. The smells you will get are grass smells, maybe a cheesy smell (lactic acid), and definitely a vinegary smell (acetic acid). It might smell a little alcoholic or like nail polish remover, too.

Don't worry – all these smells are a good sign! If you notice a foul smell, don't worry – as long as there are bubbles in the mixture, it is working.

Reviving a starter

What happens if you don't make bread using your sourdough starter for a while and it's been in the fridge for a long time? Well, the coldness of the fridge slows down the process of fermentation and the mixture goes to sleep. You may also find that it will have separated and a grey/brown liquid might form on top. It'll probably have a strong vinegar smell but it's safe to taste (it will be very sour though). Your first reaction will be to throw it away, but it can be saved. Remove the liquid or the mould. Start building up the starter slowly, by adding just 2 g/ 2 ml/½ teaspoon of the mixture from the jar and 20 g/4 tablespoons flour and 20 g/20 ml/4 teaspoons water. Leave in a warm place for 8 hours, then repeat, and build it up until it is nice and bubbly, as before. **Remember that if the sourdough is not bubbling, the bread will not rise**. Once you've built it up, throw away the rest of the old starter and replace it with the new one in a clean jar. Always build up the starter so that you have enough for your recipe and a little bit left for next time.

How to make a white sourdough starter

Day 1 In a clean jam jar, mix together 1 teaspoon of flour and 1–2 teaspoons of warm water with an ice cream stick or wooden skewer. Leave to stand overnight in a warm place.

Day 2 Add another 1 teaspoon of flour and 1–2 teaspoons of warm water to the mixture. When you open the container smell the mixture. It should just smell like flour and water mixed together, depending on what type of flour you've used. Its consistency should be that of a thick-ish batter. If the mixture is too soft, add less water next time.

Day 3 Repeat the Day 2 instructions and leave in a warm place overnight.

Day 4 Repeat the instructions from Day 2 again, leaving it in a warm place overnight. Little bubbles should be forming and it should have a slight vinegary smell.

Day 5 The mixture is now bubbling nicely, so it's ready to use (if it's not bubbling like it is in the image below, add another teaspoon of flour and 2 teaspoons of water and check it the next day). You can now build up your sourdough. Put the sourdough starter into a large mixing bowl, and add 100g/¾ cup flour. Add 100 g/100 ml/ 7 tablespoons warm water to the large mixing bowl and mix together. Cover the bowl with a shower cap and leave to ferment overnight in a warm place.

The benefits of sourdough

Sourdough bread takes longer to make than factory-produced bread. But unlike the homogenized rectangular lumps that we see piled high on supermarket shelves, there is a magic and a beauty to the making of sourdough. It is the way bread used to be made, and the love and time that goes into making it is rewarded with a depth of flavour and texture that is incomparable. It even grows old gracefully and tastes good stale. These aren't the only rewards, however. Mounting evidence suggests that long-fermented bread may be easier to digest and provide a number of health benefits.

Sourdough bread is more nutritious and easier to digest than regular loaves. The naturally occurring lactobacilli (lactic acid bacteria) helps to reduce the rate at which glucose enters the bloodstream. This means that sourdough does not cause a rapid spike in insulin levels, and therefore it possesses a relatively low glycaemic index (G.I.). The lactic acid bacteria, as well as giving sourdough bread its wonderfully sour tang, also improves the digestibility of gluten, reducing the likelihood of developing an intolerance to the bread.

Cases of diabetes, the disease characterized by the body's inability to regulate the amount of sugar in the bloodstream, have experienced a 60 per cent increase in the UK alone in the past 10 years. Incidences of the most severe form of gluten sensitivity, coeliac/celiac disease, have risen rapidly over the last few decades. Cases of less severe forms of gluten sensitivity have also surged, causing a variety of digestive problems. The fact that mass-produced bread contains added gluten may be more than just a coincidence. However, it may not come as a surprise that people making the switch from processed bread to sourdough often experience reduced digestive discomfort. This is likely to be because gluten is broken down during sourdough's fermentation process, making it practically innocuous. An Italian scientific study, published in 2011 in the journal *Clinical Gastroenterology and Hepatology*, backs up this claim. It demonstrated that 60 coeliac/celiac patients who were fed sourdough bread for 60 days experienced no clinical complaints. Biopsies of their intestinal lining showed no changes. More work needs to be done in this area, but it is certainly a significant discovery.

The positive effect on the structure of gluten is just one of the benefits of the long-fermentation process. It also makes vital nutrients and minerals much simpler for our bodies to absorb, including iron, zinc, magnesium, B-vitamins, folic acid and a number of antioxidants. This is mainly due to the fact that lactic acid bacteria, which develops in the sourdough, helps to neutralize phytates (acids that bond to important minerals, reducing the body's ability to absorb them).

A selection of sourdough starters
Top row: light rye, barley, maize, emmer
Second row: brown rice, chickpea/gram, wholemeal/wholewheat, oat
Third row: teff, white, quinoa, kamut
Bottom row: einkorn, dark rye, buckwheat, wholemeal/wholewheat spelt

Experimenting with starters

One of the excitements of choosing recipes for this book has been experimenting with different sourdough starters. One of these is raisin water, which can be made by adding a handful of raisins to about 200 g/200 ml/¾ cup of warm water (30–37°C/86–99°F) in a kilner jar. Keep it in a warm place, and open the jar every 8 hours or so to let in some air and to see how it is coming along. In a few days, the mixture will be bubbling and fizzing. It's very important that the mixture bubbles and fizzes before using it.

To turn raisin water into a beer barm (starter), which you can use a substitute for beer barm in all but one of the recipes in the Cultured Sourdoughs chapter, take 1 part raisin water (no raisins, though) and 1 part plain malt (Maris Otter), mix together and leave it to ferment for 2–3 hours. By then the mixture will start bubbling and fizzing. Take the malted raisin water and mix it with flour, using equal parts of malted raisin water and flour. Leave this to ferment overnight and you'll have enough to use in a starter the following day. When you're not using it, keep it in the fridge.

E

Making the dough

The instructions on pages 20–31 teach you, step-by-step, how to make a plain white sourdough loaf, from kneading the dough to shaping different kinds of loaves. You will first need to read the information on how to make and how to build up a sourdough starter on pages 16–17, as this is the crucial first stage in making a sourdough loaf. However, if you already have a sourdough starter, you can make and bake this loaf on the same day. Follow the instructions on pages 20–23, but use 180 g/6½ oz. active sourdough starter instead of 30 g/2 tablespoons and leave the dough to rest in a warm place for 1 hour rather than overnight. Then follow the instructions on pages 24–27 to make a round loaf or follow the instructions on pages 28–31 to make a long loaf.

1 In a small mixing bowl, mix the flour and salt together thoroughly and set aside. This is the dry mixture. Note that when weighing out dry ingredients, it's a good idea to put the smaller ingredients on top, so that you can keep track of the ingredients you're using. **(A)**

2 Weigh the sourdough starter into a large mixing bowl.

3 Weigh out the warm water in a measuring jug/pitcher and transfer ¾ of it into your large mixing bowl with the weighed-out sourdough starter. We use ¾ of the water because different flours absorb slightly different amounts of water. **(B)**

4 Dissolve or break up the sourdough starter in the water.

5 Once the sourdough starter has dissolved, add the dry mixture **(C)** and stir the mixture slowly with your hands until it comes together **(D)**. Use a plastic dough scraper to scrape the sides of the bowl so that no dry bits of dough form here. **(E)**

6 If the dough doesn't come together and it seems a bit dry, add a little or all of the remaining water you weighed out in the measuring jug/pitcher in step 3.

7 At this point the dough should come together and be slightly sticky. If it is still a bit dry and you have put all the water into the mixture, add some more water, remembering to record how much you have added for next time.

8 Cover the mixture with the small mixing bowl that contained the dry mixture.

9 Leave to stand for 10 minutes.

TIME PLANNER

Building up the sourdough **8 hours** (see page 17)

Making the dough **50 minutes**

Letting the dough rise **12–24 hours** (depending on how warm the place is where it is left to rise)

Knocking back and shaping the dough **10 minutes**

Final proofing **2–6 hours** (depending on how warm the place is where it is left to proof)

Resting in the fridge before baking **30 minutes**

Baking **30–40 minutes**

Cooling **30 minutes**

INGREDIENTS

600 g/4 cups white strong/ bread flour, plus extra for dusting

12 g/2¼ teaspoons salt

30 g/2 tablespoons sourdough starter (see pages 16–17)

360 g/360 ml/1½ cups warm water (30–37°C/86–99°F)

EQUIPMENT

1 x 800-g/1¾-lbs. proofing/ dough-rising basket or 1 x 800-g/1¾-lbs. loaf pan, greased with vegetable or sunflower oil

1 small peel, floured, for loading the loaf into the oven (if using a proofing/dough-rising basket)

Makes 1 x 800-g/1¾-lbs. loaf

Kneading the dough

The dough requires kneading in order to strengthen it. I believe in a very basic method of kneading. The dough is effectively folded inside the mixing bowl 10 times and for about 10 seconds. We do this 10-second kneading process 4 times in total with 10 minutes of rest in between each stage. In this 10 minutes, the gluten relaxes, which makes it easy to knead. The flour also has time to absorb the liquid. I always make a small indentation in the dough with my finger to keep track of how many stages of kneading it has been through.

1 After 10 minutes, the dough is ready to be kneaded. Leaving it in the bowl, start by squashing the dough with your knuckles and fingers to flatten out any lumps. It should now look pancake-shaped. **(A)**

2 Lift a portion of the dough up from the side and fold it into the middle and press with your knuckles. **(B)**

3 Turn the bowl 90° clockwise and lift another portion of the dough up from the side and fold it into the middle and press with your knuckles.

4 Repeat steps 2 and 3 another 8 times (10 folds in total). You have now kneaded the dough once. The whole process should only take about 10 seconds and the dough should start to resist. If the dough starts to resist and starts to tear, apply less pressure to the dough as you knead. Also, if you can only knead the dough 8 times before it starts to resist (making it difficult to continue kneading), then stop. **(C)**

5 Turn the ball of dough over in the bowl and make a finger mark in the dough (to indicate the first knead) **(D)**. Cover with the bowl that had the dry mixture in it. **(E)**

6 Leave the dough to rest for 10 minutes.

7 Turn the dough over and repeat steps 2–6 another time so that the dough has a second finger mark **(F)**. After the second kneading, the dough should resist strongly when you pull it.

8 Repeat steps 2–6 again, remembering to make another finger mark (the third finger mark) **(G)**. After the third kneading, the dough should be beautifully smooth.

9 Repeat steps 2–6 a final time **(H) (I) (J) (K)** and remember to make the fourth and final finger mark **(L)**. Leave the dough to rise overnight.

Note: If you find the dough is too sticky, dip your fingers in flour each time you knead. If you find the dough is a bit dry, dip your hand in water (shaking off the excess water) each time you knead.

A   B   C

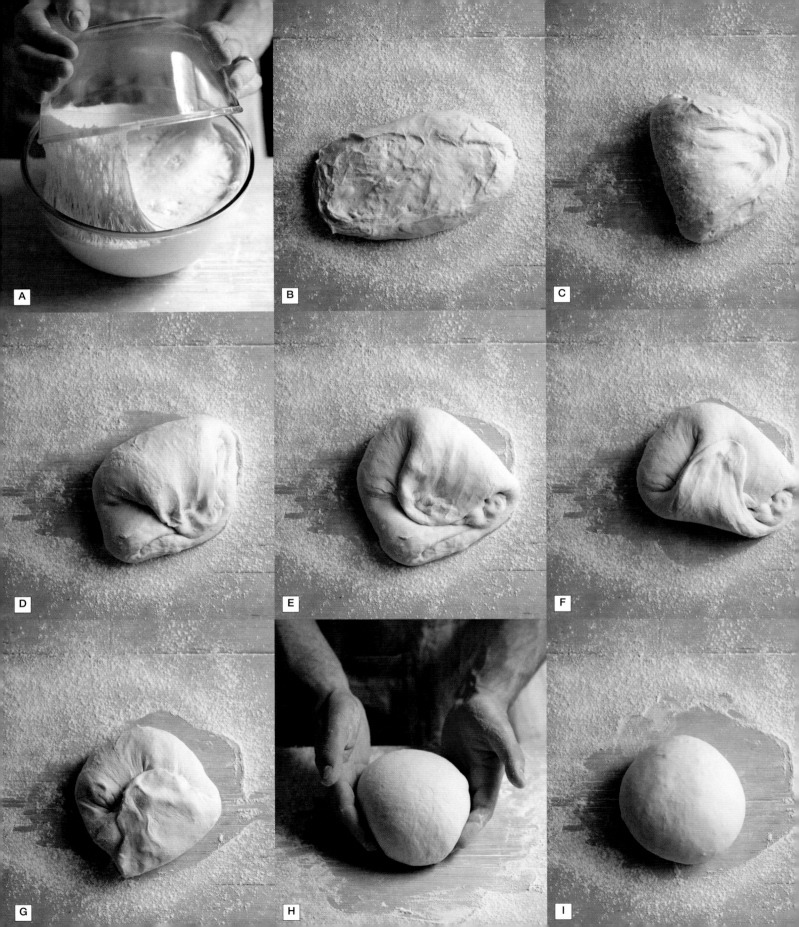

Shaping a round loaf

1 The next day, the dough will have increased in volume. Remove the bowl covering the dough **(A)**. Clench your hand into a fist and gently punch down the centre of the dough to release the trapped air.

2 Remove the dough from the bowl, using a light sprinkling of white flour so the dough does not stick. **(B)**

3 Flatten the dough slightly with your palm.

4 Take a corner of the dough and fold it right over to the opposite side then turn the dough 90° clockwise. **(C)**

5 Repeat the previous step 4–5 more times until the dough is a roundish shape. **(D) (E) (F) (G)**

6 Turn the dough over and tuck in the underneath of the dough with your fingers as you rotate the dough clockwise until you've formed a rounded ball **(H) (I)**. Make sure you remove the flour from the dough's surface.

7 Sprinkle the dough with flour **(J)** and coat the inside of a round proofing/dough-rising basket with flour.

8 Flatten the rounded ball slightly with the palm of your hand so that it fits nicely in the proofing/dough-rising basket. **(K) (L)**

9 The dough is now ready for the proofing stage. You will need a warm place to allow the dough to rise in. I preheat my oven to 50°C (120°F), and once the oven reaches that temperature, I place the loaf inside. Make sure that you turn the oven off, though.

Proofing and baking a round loaf

1 Allow to rise in a warm place for 2–6 hours or until the dough has nearly doubled in volume **(A)**. Cover with a shower cap or with a mixing bowl only if a skin starts to form.

2 Preheat the oven to 250°C (500°F) Gas 9. Place a roasting tray at the bottom and a baking sheet on the middle shelf.

3 If using a proofing/dough-rising basket, place it in the fridge for 30 minutes to stabilize the dough.

4 If you have a Dutch oven, sprinkle the cold base with flour and transfer the dough into it **(B) (C)**. Or, tip the dough out of the proofing/dough-rising basket and onto a floured peel.

5 Slash the loaf with a sharp serrated knife or a lamé with a design of your choice. **(D)**

6 Slide the loaf onto the preheated baking sheet in the oven. Pour a cup of water into the roasting tray and lower the temperature to 220°C (425°F) Gas 7. If using a Dutch oven, replace the lid **(E)** and transfer to the oven. Note that you don't need to add a cup of water if using a Dutch oven.

7 Bake for 30–40 minutes until golden brown. If using a Dutch oven, remove the lid for the last 10 minutes **(F)**. Tap the bottom of the loaf – it should sound hollow. Let cool on a wire rack.

A B C
D E F

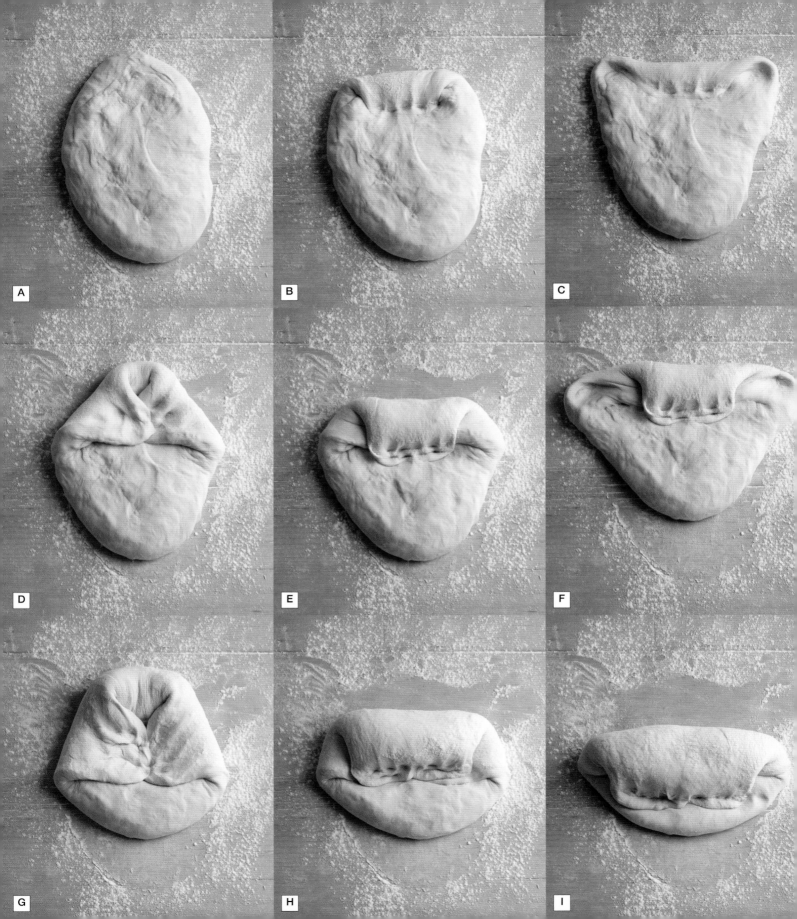

Shaping a long loaf

1 The next day, the dough will have increased in volume. Remove the bowl covering the dough. Clench your hand into a fist and gently punch down the centre of the dough to release the trapped air.

2 Transfer the dough to a lightly floured surface using a plastic dough scraper. If the dough is sticky, coat it in a little flour. Shape the dough into an oval and flatten the surface. **(A)**

3 Take the top of the dough and fold it over slightly to make the top edge straighter **(B)**. Take both corners of the top side of the dough and stretch them out slightly. **(C)**

4 Take the top right corner and fold it to the middle of the dough, then do the same with the left-hand side of the dough. The top of the dough will look triangular. **(D)**

5 Take the point of the 'triangle' and fold it back over to the middle of the dough. **(E)**

6 Elongate the top corners of the dough again. **(F)**

7 Fold the elongated top corners back into the middle of the dough again. **(G)**

8 Take the top part of the dough and fold it back to the middle so that it forms a roll. **(H)**

9 Roll the roll-shape towards you a little more. **(I)**

10 Use the tips of your fingers to straighten and tighten the roll of dough and form it into a Swiss/jelly-roll shape. **(J)**

11 Press both sides of the top and the bottom of the loaf to create a slightly more tapered shape. **(K)**

12 Sprinkle the top of the loaf with flour. It's now ready to place into a greased loaf pan or floured long proofing/dough-rising basket. **(L)**

J

K

L

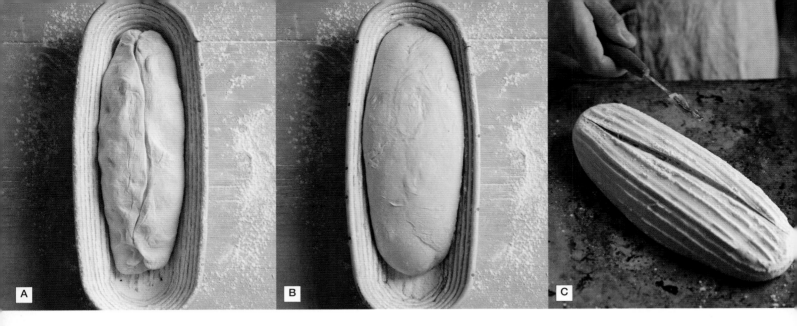

A

B

C

Proofing and baking a long loaf

1 Place the loaf seam-up into a floured proofing/dough-rising basket **(A)**. Alternatively, place the loaf seam-down into a greased loaf pan.

2 Allow to proof for 2–6 hours or until the dough has doubled in size **(B)**. If the loaf is in a proofing/dough-rising basket and a skin starts to form, cover it with a shower cap. If you're going to be baking the loaf in a loaf pan, cover it with a shower cap.

3 Preheat the oven to 250°C (500°F) Gas 9 and place a deep roasting tray on the bottom shelf of the oven. If using a loaf pan, place a baking sheet on the middle shelf of the oven.

4 If the dough is in the proofing/dough-rising basket, place the proofing/dough-rising basket in the fridge for 30 minutes to stabilize the dough. If the loaf is in a loaf pan, it does not need to go in the fridge. However, if the oven is not ready, place the loaf in the fridge to prevent it from over-proofing.

5 Turn the loaf out of the proofing/dough-rising basket and onto a floured peel. If you're using a loaf pan, don't worry about this stage.

6 Slash the loaf with a sharp serrated knife or a lamé with a design of your choice. **(C)**

7 Place the loaf pan, or slide the loaf onto the baking sheet, in the preheated oven. Pour a cup of water into the hot roasting tray to form steam. This will help create a nice crust. Lower the temperature to 220°C (425°F) Gas 7.

8 Bake for 30–40 minutes until golden brown. Tip the loaf upside-down and tap the bottom – it should sound hollow. If not, return it in the oven for 10 minutes. Remove the loaf and allow to cool on a wire rack.

WHOLEGRAIN AND ANCIENT GRAIN SOURDOUGHS

Wholemeal sourdough

This classic, simple wholemeal/wholewheat loaf is a good one to start with. All it takes to make it look really attractive is a couple of slashes after the proofing stage. Bear in mind that different brands of wholemeal/wholewheat flour will require different amounts of water when making this loaf.

TIME PLANNER

Making the dough
50 minutes

Letting the dough rise
12–24 hours

Knocking back and shaping
the dough **10 minutes**

Final proofing **2–6 hours**

Resting in the fridge
30 minutes

Baking **30–40 minutes**

Cooling **30 minutes**

INGREDIENTS

500 g/4 cups wholemeal/
wholewheat flour, plus extra
for dusting

10 g/2 teaspoons salt

25 g/1 oz. wholemeal/
wholewheat sourdough
starter (see pages 16–17)

380 g/380 ml/1½ cups warm
water (30–37°C/86–99°F)

EQUIPMENT

1 x 800-g/1¾-lbs. round
proofing/dough-rising
basket

1 small peel, floured

**Makes 1 x 800-g/1¾-lbs.
loaf**

1 In a small mixing bowl, mix the flour and salt together thoroughly. Set aside. This is the dry mixture.

2 Add the sourdough starter to a large mixing bowl. Add ¾ of the water and dissolve or break up the sourdough with your hands.

3 Add the dry mixture. Stir the mixture slowly with your hands until it comes together and there are no dry bits at the bottom of the bowl.

4 Add the remaining water. If the mixture doesn't come together and it seems a bit dry, add more water and record how much you used for next time. The dough should be slightly sticky.

5 Cover the mixture with the small mixing bowl that contained the flour mixture. Leave to stand for 10 minutes.

6 Knead the mixture 10 times (see page 22).

7 Turn the ball of dough over in the bowl and make a finger mark in the dough (to indicate the first knead).

8 Cover with the small mixing bowl again and leave the dough to rest for 10 minutes.

9 Repeat steps 6–8 another 3 times, making sure the mixture is covered between kneads and remembering to mark the dough indicating the amount of kneads done.

10 Cover the dough and leave it to rise overnight in a cool place (not in the fridge, though).

11 The next day, gently punch down to de-gas the dough.

12 Remove from the bowl, using a light sprinkling of flour so the dough does not stick. Shape the dough into a ball (see pages 24–25).

13 Coat the proofing/dough-rising basket with flour. Coat the top of the dough with flour and place seam-up into the basket.

14 Allow to proof for 2–6 hours or until the dough has nearly doubled in volume. Cover with a shower cap or with an upturned mixing bowl if a skin starts to form.

15 Place the dough in the fridge for 30 minutes to stabilize it.

16 Preheat the oven to 250°C (500°F) Gas 9. Place a deep roasting tray at the bottom of the oven and a baking sheet on the middle shelf.

17 Turn the dough out onto a floured peel.

18 Slash the loaf with a sharp serrated knife or a lamé with a design of your own choice.

19 Slide the loaf onto the preheated baking sheet in the oven. Pour a cup of water into the hot roasting tray and lower the temperature to 220°C (425°F) Gas 7.

20 Bake for 30–40 minutes until golden brown.

21 Tap the loaf on the bottom. If you hear a hollow sound, it is ready. If you are not sure, return it to the oven for a further 10 minutes.

22 Remove the loaf from the baking sheet and allow it to cool on a wire rack.

Seeded wholemeal sourdough

Loaded with omega-3, this nutty-tasting loaf looks great, with the oatmeal coating toasting nicely. Sunflower or pumpkin seeds can be used as alternatives for two of the seeds listed.

A

B

TIME PLANNER

Making the seed soaker
30 minutes

Making the dough
50 minutes

Letting the dough rise
8–12 hours

Knocking back and shaping the dough
10 minutes

Final proofing 2–6 hours

Baking 30–40 minutes

Cooling 30 minutes

INGREDIENTS

30 g/¼ cup sesame seeds

30 g/¼ cup linseeds

10 g/1½ tablespoons hemp seeds (hulled)

100 g/100 ml/ 7 tablespoons boiling water

400 g/3 cups wholemeal/ wholewheat flour

8 g/1½ teaspoons salt

20 g/¾ oz. sourdough starter (see pages 16–17)

250 g/250 ml/1 cup warm water (30–37°C/86–99°F)

coarse oatmeal, for coating the loaf

EQUIPMENT

1 x 800-g/1¾-lbs. long proofing/dough-rising basket

1 proofing/baker's linen or tea/dish towel, for lining the proofing/ dough-rising basket

1 small peel, floured

Makes 1 x 800-g/ 1¾-lbs. loaf

1 In a small mixing bowl, soak all the seeds in the boiling water for 30 minutes. Ensure that the water covers the seeds. **(A)**

2 In a small mixing bowl, mix the flour and salt together thoroughly with a wooden spoon. This is the dry mixture.

3 Add the sourdough starter to a large mixing bowl with ¾ of the warm water. Add the soaked seeds and mix together.

4 Once the sourdough has dissolved, add the dry mixture. Stir the mixture slowly with your hands until it comes together and there are no dry bits at the bottom of the bowl.

5 At this point the dough should come together and be slightly sticky. Add more of the remaining water if needed. Cover with the small mixing bowl and leave to stand for 10 minutes.

6 Knead the mixture 10 times (see page 22).

7 Turn the ball of dough over in the bowl and make a finger mark in the dough (to indicate the first knead).

8 Cover with the small mixing bowl again and leave the dough to rest for 10 minutes.

9 Repeat steps 6–8 another 3 times, making sure the mixture is covered between kneads and remembering to mark the dough to indicate the number of kneads done.

10 Cover the dough and leave it to rise for 8–12 hours in a cool place (not in the fridge, though).

11 After 8–12 hours, gently punch down to de-gas the dough.

12 Line a long proofing/dough-rising basket with a proofing/baker's linen or clean tea/dish towel. Sprinkle coarse oatmeal into the proofing/dough-rising basket.

13 Remove from the bowl, using a light sprinkling of flour so the dough does not stick. Shape the dough into a long loaf (see pages 28–29). Coat the top with flour and place the loaf seam-up into a floured long proofing/dough-rising basket.

14 Roll the top of the loaf on a damp tea/dish towel to make it sticky, then roll it in the coarse oatmeal again, making sure that the top and sides are covered.

15 Place the loaf seam-up into the proofing/dough-rising basket.

16 Allow to proof for 2–6 hours or until the dough has nearly doubled in volume. **(B)**

17 Preheat the oven to 250°C (500°F) Gas 9. Place a deep roasting tray at the bottom of the oven and a baking sheet on the middle shelf.

18 Turn the dough out onto a floured peel.

19 Slide the loaf onto the preheated baking sheet in the oven. Pour a cup of water into the hot roasting tray and lower the temperature to 220°C (425°F) Gas 7.

20 Bake for 30–40 minutes until golden brown.

21 Tap the loaf on the bottom. If you hear a hollow sound, it is ready. If you are not sure, return it to the oven for a further 10 minutes.

22 Remove the loaf from the baking sheet and allow it to cool on a wire rack.

Barley and rye sourdough

Barley is not commonly used in baking, but it makes for a really tasty loaf when combined with rye. This bread tastes best the day after you have baked it and goes well with savoury or sweet toppings.

TIME PLANNER

Making the pre-ferment
8 hours

Soaking the pearl barley
8 hours

Making and shaping the dough **15 minutes**

Final proofing **1–2 hours**

Baking **30–40 minutes**

Cooling **30 minutes**

INGREDIENTS

150 g/¾ cup pearl barley

200 g/1½ cups barley flour

6 g/1 teaspoon salt

150 g/150 ml/⅔ cup hot water (just boiled)

dark rye flour, for topping

For the pre-ferment

150 g/1¼ cups dark rye flour, plus extra for topping the loaf

100 g/3½ oz. rye sourdough starter (see pages 16–17)

200 g/200 ml/¾ cup cold water

EQUIPMENT

1 x 500-g/1-lb. loaf pan, greased with vegetable or sunflower oil

Makes 1 x 800-g/1¾-lbs. loaf

1 To make the pre-ferment, add the dark rye flour, the rye sourdough starter and the cold water to a large mixing bowl and mix with a wooden spoon. Leave to ferment at room temperature for 8 hours or overnight, covered with a small mixing bowl acting as a lid.

2 Meanwhile, in a large mixing bowl, soak the pearl barley for 8 hours or overnight in about two times its volume of warm water.

3 The next day (or after 8 hours), prepare the dough. In another small mixing bowl, mix the barley flour and salt together and set aside. This is the dry mixture.

4 Pass the pearl barley through a sieve/strainer to drain the excess water.

5 Add the dry mixture to the bubbling pre-ferment. Add the drained pot barely and the hot water.

6 Mix with a wooden spoon until it is thoroughly mixed together.

7 Put the mixture into the greased loaf pan and shape using a plastic dough scraper. Sprinkle some extra dark rye flour on the surface and slash the top with a sharp serrated knife or a lamé to decorate.

8 Cover with the large mixing bowl or a shower cap and allow to rise for 1–2 hours. You will know when it is ready because cracks and little air holes will appear on the floured surface. Don't let it rise too much as it will overflow over the loaf pan.

9 Preheat the oven to 250°C (500°F) Gas 9 and place a deep roasting tray at the bottom of the oven.

10 Remove the large bowl or shower cap that has been covering the loaf and place the loaf pan in the preheated oven.

11 Pour a cup of water into the hot roasting tray and lower the temperature to 220°C (425°F) Gas 7.

12 Bake for 30–40 minutes until golden brown.

13 Tap the loaf on the bottom. If you hear a hollow sound, it is ready. If you are not sure, return it to the oven for a further 10 minutes.

14 Turn the loaf out of the loaf pan and allow it to cool on a wire rack.

A

B

Sourdough oat cans

Oats are a rich source of soluble fibre and magnesium. So why not bake a healthy loaf in a fun, easy way – by using cleaned tin cans. Once baked, cut into rounds and toast it. Serve simply with butter or with a selection of cheeses and chutney – it's a magic combination.

1 To make the pre-ferment, add the fine oatmeal, the oat flour sourdough starter and the warm water to a large mixing bowl and mix with a wooden spoon. Leave to ferment for 8 hours or overnight, covered with a small mixing bowl acting as a lid.

2 The next day (or after 8 hours), prepare the dough. In another small mixing bowl, mix the fine oatmeal, lightly toasted porridge/rolled oats and salt together and set aside. This is the dry mixture.

3 Add the dry mixture to the bubbling pre-ferment and add the warm water.

4 Mix with a wooden spoon until it is thoroughly mixed together.

5 Lightly grease the inside of the cans with butter and coat them with fine oatmeal flour.

6 Put the mixture into the cans and shape using a plastic dough scraper or a spoon. Sprinkle with more flour. **(A)**

7 Cover with a large mixing bowl and allow to rise for 2–4 hours. You will know when they are ready because cracks and little holes will appear on the surface. The dough should rise to 1–2 cm/½–¾ inch above the cans.

8 Preheat the oven to 250°C (500°F) Gas 9 and place a deep roasting tray at the bottom of the oven.

9 Remove the bowl and place the cans in the preheated oven.

10 Pour a cup of water into the hot roasting tray and lower the temperature to 220°C (425°F) Gas 7.

11 Bake for 15–20 minutes until golden brown. **(B)**

12 Turn the loaves out of the cans and allow to cool on a wire rack.

TIME PLANNER

Making the pre-ferment **8 hours**

Making and shaping the dough **15 minutes**

Final proofing **2–4 hours**

Baking **15–20 minutes**

Cooling **30 minutes**

INGREDIENTS

150 g/1½ cups fine oatmeal, plus extra for dusting

150 g/1½ cups porridge/rolled oats, lightly toasted

8 g/1½ teaspoons salt

180 g/180 ml/¾ cup warm water (30–37°C/86–99°F)

For the pre-ferment

150 g/1½ cups fine oatmeal, plus extra for coating the tins

70 g/2½ oz. oat flour sourdough starter (see pages 16–17)

150 g/150 ml/½ cup plus 2 tablespoons warm water (30–37°C/86–99°F)

EQUIPMENT

2 x 400-g/14-oz. tin cans or 4 x 200-g/7-oz. tin cans, buttered

Makes 2 x 400-g/14-oz. or 4 x 200-g/7-oz. 'canned' loaves

Pumpernickel sourdough

This rich, intense and filling loaf contains three colourful, aromatic grains that you may need to find online or in speciality shops, but the wait will be worth it. Pumpernickel will keep for many days after baking. It goes especially well topped with smoked salmon and cream cheese.

TIME PLANNER

Soaking the rye grains **8 hours**

Making the dough **15 minutes**

Letting the dough rise **8 hours**

Shaping the dough **15 minutes**

Final proofing **4–8 hours**

Baking **1 hour**

Cooling **30 minutes**

INGREDIENTS

100 g/⅔ cup rye grains

20 g/4 teaspoons dark malt (chocolate malt), crushed

40 g/¼ cup crystal malt, crushed

40 g/¼ cup plain malt (Maris Otter), crushed

250 g/1½ cups chopped rye

5 g/1 teaspoon salt

250 g/9 oz. rye sourdough starter (see pages 16–17)

250 g/250 ml/1 cup warm water (30–37°C/86–99°F)

EQUIPMENT

1 x 800-g/1¾-lbs. loaf pan, greased with vegetable or sunflower oil

Makes 1 x 800-g/1¾-lbs. loaf

1 Soak the rye grains overnight in a bowl.

2 In a small mixing bowl, mix the 3 types of malted grain (the dark malt, crystal malt and pale malt), chopped rye and salt together thoroughly. This is the dry mixture. **(A)**

3 In a large mixing bowl, add the sourdough starter, the warm water and the dry mixture. Mix thoroughly with a wooden spoon. **(B)**

4 Cover with the small mixing bowl and leave to rise overnight.

5 The next morning, transfer the mixture into the greased loaf pan and shape using a plastic dough scraper **(C)**. Cover with the large mixing bowl or a shower cap.

6 Allow the mixture to rest for 4–8 hours until fully proofed. You will know when it is ready because cracks and little air holes will appear on the floured surface. **(D)**

7 Preheat the oven to 250°C (500°F) Gas 9 and place a deep roasting tray at the bottom of the oven.

8 Remove the large bowl or shower cap and place the loaf pan in the preheated oven, covered by a baking sheet.

9 Pour a cup of water into the hot roasting tray and lower the temperature to 200°C (400°F) Gas 6.

10 Bake for 60 minutes until baked through. Remove the baking sheet that is covering the loaf pan.

11 Turn the bread out of the loaf pan and tap it on the bottom. If you hear a hollow sound, it is ready. If you are not sure, return it to the oven for a further 10 minutes.

12 I normally place a bowl over the hot loaf so that it can sweat. This will help keep some of the moisture in the loaf. When cool, uncover and serve.

A B C D

Spelt or kamut sourdough

Making the pre-ferment
8 hours

Soaking the grains **8 hours**

Making the dough **15 minutes**

Final proofing **2–6 hours**

Baking **30–40 minutes**

Cooling **30 minutes**

INGREDIENTS

120 g/4½ oz. spelt or kamut grains

110 g/1 scant cup reserved cooking water (if making spelt bread) and 150 g/150 ml/⅔ cup reserved cooking water (if making kamut bread)

160 g/1¼ cups wholemeal/wholewheat spelt flour or wholemeal/wholewheat kamut flour

10 g/2 teaspoons salt

For the pre-ferment

12 g/⅖ oz. spelt or kamut sourdough starter (see pages 16–17)

120 g/120 ml/½ cup warm water (30–37°C/86–99°F)

120 g/1 scant cup wholemeal/wholewheat spelt or wholemeal/wholewheat kamut flour

EQUIPMENT

1 x 500-g/1-lb. loaf pan, greased with vegetable or sunflower oil

Makes 1 x 800-g/1¾-lbs. loaf

Two ancient grains, spelt and kamut, have become popular because they taste great and are very easy to digest after soaking. The legend goes that kamut grains were found in the tomb of an Ancient Egyptian Pharaoh, so it became known as 'King Tut's wheat'. The recipes are slightly different because kamut absorbs more water than spelt.

1 To make the pre-ferment, add the spelt or kamut sourdough starter and the warm water to a large mixing bowl. Add the spelt or kamut flour and mix until all is combined. Scrape the sides of the bowl using a plastic dough scraper and leave to ferment for 8 hours or overnight, covered with a small mixing bowl acting as a lid.

2 Meanwhile, in a large mixing bowl, soak the spelt or kamut grains for 8 hours or overnight in about 3 times their volume of water until they are soft. **(A)**

3 The next day (or after 8 hours), boil the spelt or kamut grains in a saucepan with enough water to cover the grains. Cook for 10 minutes or until soft, adding some more water to cover the grains while they are cooking.

4 Once the grains are soft, remove from the heat and leave to cool in the saucepan before passing through a sieve/strainer and reserving the water.

5 Add the spelt or kamut flour and the salt to a small mixing bowl, mix them both together and set aside. This is the dry mixture.

6 Pour the dry mixture onto the bubbling pre-ferment. Add the cooked cooled spelt or kamut grains and 110 g/110 ml/1 scant cup of the reserved water if making a spelt loaf and 150 g/150 ml/⅔ cup of the reserved water if making a kamut loaf.

7 Mix everything together until it forms a porridge/oatmeal consistency.

8 Transfer the mixture into a greased loaf pan. Dip a plastic dough scraper or a metal spoon into some water, and use either one to shape the loaf.

9 Cover with a large mixing bowl or a shower cap and allow to rise for 2–6 hours. You will know when it is ready because cracks and little air holes will appear on the surface. **(B: spelt, left; kamut, right)**

10 Preheat the oven to 250°C (500°F) Gas 9 and place a deep roasting tray at the bottom of the oven.

11 Remove the large bowl or shower cap that has been covering the loaf and place the pan in the preheated oven.

12 Pour a cup of water into the hot roasting tray and lower the temperature to 220°C (425°F) Gas 7.

13 Bake for 30–40 minutes until golden brown.

14 Tap the loaf on the bottom. If you hear a hollow sound, it is ready. If you are not sure, leave it in the oven for a further 10 minutes.

15 Turn the loaf out of the loaf pan and allow it to cool on a wire rack.

Spelt and sprouted spelt flour sourdough

Spelt is a particularly popular grain at the moment and is increasingly found in supermarkets and grocery stores as well as health food shops. The sprouted spelt flour gives it a different dimension, adding a nice bit of sweetness. Bear in mind that the dough will be slightly stiffer than a normal white dough.

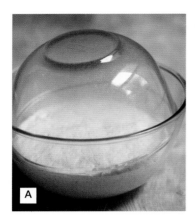

A

TIME PLANNER

Making the dough **50 minutes**

Letting the dough rise
12–24 hours

Knocking back and shaping the dough **10 minutes**

Final proofing **2–6 hours**

Resting in the fridge **30 minutes**

Baking **30–40 minutes**

Cooling **30 minutes**

INGREDIENTS

500 g/3¾ cups white spelt flour, plus extra for dusting

100 g/¾ cup sprouted spelt flour

10 g/2 teaspoons salt

30 g/1 oz. sourdough starter (see pages 16–17)

300 g/300 ml/1¼ cups warm water (30–37°C/86–99°F)

EQUIPMENT

1 x 800-g/1¾-lb. round proofing/dough-rising basket

Makes 1 x 800-g/1¾-lbs. loaf

1 In a small mixing bowl, mix the white spelt flour, sprouted spelt flour and salt together thoroughly and set aside. This is the dry mixture.

2 Weigh the sourdough starter into a large mixing bowl. Add ¾ of the water and dissolve or break up the sourdough.

3 Add the dry mixture. Stir the mixture slowly with your hands until it comes together and there are no dry bits at the bottom of the bowl.

4 If the mixture doesn't come together and it seems a bit dry, add some of the remaining water. The dough should be slightly sticky.

5 Cover the mixture with the small mixing bowl that had the flour mixture in it. Leave to stand for 10 minutes.

6 Knead the mixture 10 times (see page 22).

7 Turn the ball of dough over in the bowl and make a finger mark in the dough (to indicate the first knead).

8 Cover with the small mixing bowl again and leave the dough to rest for 10 minutes.

9 Repeat steps 6–8 another 3 times, making sure the mixture is covered between kneads and remembering to mark the dough to indicate the number of kneads done. If the dough starts to resist and starts to tear apply less pressure as you knead. If the dough becomes difficult to knead after kneading it 8 times, stop.

10 Cover the dough and leave it to rise overnight in a cool place (not in the fridge, though). **(A)**

11 The next day, gently punch down to de-gas the dough.

12 Remove from the bowl, using a light sprinkling of spelt flour so the dough does not stick.

13 Shape the dough into a ball. First, flatten the dough slightly with your palm.

14 Take a corner of the dough and fold it right over to the opposite side, then turn the dough 90° clockwise.

15 Repeat the previous step 4–5 more times until the dough is a roundish shape. Turn the dough over and keep tucking in the underneath of the dough with your fingers as you rotate the dough clockwise, until you've formed a rounded ball.

16 Coat the proofing/dough-rising basket and the top of the dough with spelt flour. Place the dough, seam-up, into the proofing/dough-rising basket.

17 Allow to proof for 2–6 hours or until the dough has almost doubled in volume. Cover only if a skin begins to form. **(B)**

18 Place the dough in the fridge for 30 minutes to stabilize it.

19 Preheat the oven to 250°C (500°F) Gas 9. Place a deep roasting tray at the bottom of the oven and a baking sheet on the middle shelf.

B

C

20 Turn the dough out onto a floured peel.

21 Slash the loaf with a sharp serrated knife or a lamé with a design of your own choice. **(C)**

22 Slide the loaf onto the preheated baking sheet in the oven. Pour a cup of water into the hot roasting tray and lower the temperature to 220°C (425°F) Gas 7.

23 Bake for 30–40 minutes until golden brown.

24 Tap the loaf on the bottom. If you hear a hollow sound, it is ready. If you are not sure, return it to the oven for a further 10 minutes.

25 Remove the loaf from the baking sheet and allow it to cool on a wire rack.

A

B

TIME PLANNER

Making the dough
50 minutes

Letting the dough rise
12–24 hours

Knocking back and shaping
the dough **10 minutes**

Final proofing **2–6 hours**

Resting in the fridge
30 minutes

Baking **30–40 minutes**

Cooling **30 minutes**

INGREDIENTS

500 g/4 cups
wholemeal/wholewheat
einkorn or wholemeal/
wholewheat emmer flour,
plus extra for dusting

10 g/2 teaspoons salt

25 g/1 oz. sourdough starter
(see pages 16–17)

300 g/300 ml/1¼ cups (for
einkorn) or 320 g/320 ml/
1⅓ cups (for emmer) warm
water (30–37°C/86–99°F)

EQUIPMENT

1 x 800-g/1¾-lbs. long
proofing/dough-rising
basket

1 small peel, floured

**Makes 1 x 800-g/1¾-lbs.
loaf**

Einkorn or emmer sourdough

Einkorn and emmer belong to the same family and were among the first plants to be cultivated. They are known for their flavour and digestive qualities. These two recipes are very similar, except for the slight difference in the amount of water needed. Einkorn creates a slightly lighter coloured loaf. The dough is quite sticky, because the gluten content is not as high as a regular white loaf.

1 In a small mixing bowl, mix the flour and salt together thoroughly. Set aside. This is the dry mixture.

2 Add the sourdough starter to a large mixing bowl. Add ¾ of the warm water. Dissolve or break up the sourdough with your hands .

3 Add the dry mixture. Stir the mixture slowly with your hands until it comes together and there are no dry bits at the bottom of the bowl.

4 If the mixture doesn't come together and it seems a bit dry, add some of the remaining water. The dough should be slightly sticky.

5 Cover the mixture with the small mixing bowl that had the flour mixture in it. Leave to stand for 10 minutes.

6 Knead the mixture 10 times (see page 22).

7 Turn the ball of dough over in the bowl and make a finger mark in the dough (to indicate the first knead).

8 Cover with the small mixing bowl again and leave the dough to rest for 10 minutes.

9 Repeat steps 6–8 another 3 times, making sure the mixture is covered between kneads and remembering to mark the dough to indicate the number of kneads done. You are looking for a smooth, elastic dough. If you think the dough is not kneaded enough, repeat steps 6–8 another time. The dough will be a little stiffer than the Wholemeal Sourdough (see pages 34–35), because emmer and einkorn flour do not contain as much gluten as wholemeal/wholewheat flour.

10 Cover the dough and leave it to rise overnight in a cool place (not in the fridge, though) until fully proofed. **(A)**

11 The next day, gently punch down to de-gas the dough.

12 Dust a long proofing/dough-rising basket liberally with the type of flour you're using to make the bread with.

13 Remove from the bowl, using a light sprinkling of flour so the dough does not stick. Shape the dough into a long loaf (see pages 28–29). Coat the top with flour and place the loaf seam-up into the proofing/dough-rising basket.

14 Place the loaf seam-up into the proofing/dough-rising basket. **(B)**

15 Allow to proof for 2–6 hours or until the dough has almost doubled in volume. Note that it will not rise as much as Wholemeal Sourdough, because of the lower gluten content of einkorn and emmer flour.

16 Place the dough in the fridge for 30 minutes to stabilize it.

17 Preheat the oven to 250°C (500°F) Gas 9. Place a deep roasting tray at the bottom of the oven and a baking sheet on the middle shelf.

18 Turn the dough out onto a floured peel.

19 Slash the loaf with a sharp serrated knife or a lamé with a design of your own choice.

20 Slide the loaf onto the preheated baking sheet in the oven. Pour a cup of water into the hot roasting tray and lower the temperature to 220°C (425°F) Gas 7.

21 Bake for 30–40 minutes until golden brown.

22 Tap the loaf on the bottom. If you hear a hollow sound, it is ready. If you are not sure, return it to the oven for a further 10 minutes.

23 Remove the loaf from the baking sheet and allow it to cool on a wire rack

RYE SOURDOUGHS

Dark rye sourdough

This classic loaf has a lovely, distinctive sour flavour. It won't rise as much as other loaves, and will last for at least 3–5 days. As with some of the other rye breads, it tastes best the day after baking.

TIME PLANNER

Making the pre-ferment **8 hours**

Making and shaping the dough **15 minutes**

Final proofing **1–2 hours**

Baking **30–40 minutes**

Cooling **30 minutes**

INGREDIENTS

200 g/1½ cups dark rye flour, plus extra for topping the loaf

6 g/1 teaspoon salt

150 g/150 ml/⅔ cup hot water (just boiled)

For the pre-ferment

100 g/3½ oz. rye sourdough starter (see pages 16–17)

150 g/1¼ cups dark rye flour

200 g/200 ml/¾ cup cold water

EQUIPMENT

1 x 500-g/1-lb. loaf pan, greased with vegetable or sunflower oil

Makes 1 x 800-g/1¾-lbs. loaf

1 To make the pre-ferment, add the rye sourdough starter, the dark rye flour and the cold water to a large mixing bowl and mix with a wooden spoon. Leave to ferment for 8 hours or overnight, covered with a small mixing bowl acting as a lid.

2 The next day (or after 8 hours), prepare the dough. In a small mixing bowl, mix the dark rye flour and salt together and set aside. This is the dry mixture.

3 Add the dry mixture to the bubbling pre-ferment **(A)**, add the hot water **(B)** and mix thoroughly with a wooden spoon. **(C)**

4 Put the mixture into the greased loaf pan **(D)** and shape using a plastic dough scraper. **(E)**

5 Sprinkle some extra dark rye flour on top for decoration. **(F)**

6 Cover with the large mixing bowl or a shower cap and allow to rise in a warm place (see page 25) for 1–2 hours. You will know when it is ready because cracks and little air holes will appear on the floured surface **(G)**. Don't let it rise too much as it will overflow over the loaf pan.

7 Preheat the oven to 250°C (500°F) Gas 9 and place a deep roasting tray at the bottom of the oven.

8 Remove the large bowl or shower cap that has been covering the loaf and place the loaf pan in the preheated oven.

9 Pour a cup of water into the hot roasting tray and lower the temperature to 220°C (425°F) Gas 7.

10 Bake for 30–40 minutes until golden brown.

11 Tap the loaf on the bottom. If you hear a hollow sound, it is ready. If you are not sure, return it to the oven for a further 10–15 minutes.

12 Turn the loaf out of the loaf pan and allow it to cool on a wire rack.

A   B

Olive and tomato rye sourdough

TIME PLANNER

Making the pre-ferment **8 hours**

Making and shaping the dough
15 minutes

Final proofing **1–2 hours**

Resting in the fridge **30 minutes**

Baking **30–40 minutes**

Cooling **30 minutes**

INGREDIENTS

100 g/¾ cup dark rye flour, plus
extra for dusting and topping the
loaf

3 g/½ teaspoon salt

50 g/scant ½ cup chopped olives
(I've used olives stuffed with
anchovies)

100 g/1½ cups sundried tomatoes
(reduce to 1 scant cup if they are
packed in oil)

100 g/100 ml/7 tablespoons hot
water (just boiled)

For the pre-ferment

100 g/¾ cup dark rye flour

75 g/2½ oz. rye sourdough starter
(see pages 16–17)

100 g/100 ml/7 tablespoons cold
water

EQUIPMENT

18-cm/7-inch round sandwich
pan, greased with vegetable or
sunflower oil

Makes 1 x 18-cm/7-inch loaf

Savoury rye bread is quite unusual, but the sourness of the rye, the sweetness of the tomato and the saltiness of the olives makes this a winning combination. For the best flavour and texture, eat this loaf the day after you bake it.

1 To make the pre-ferment, add the dark rye flour, the rye sourdough starter and the cold water to a large mixing bowl and mix with a wooden spoon. Leave to ferment for 8 hours or overnight, covered with a small mixing bowl acting as a lid.

2 The next day (or after 8 hours), prepare the dough. In a small mixing bowl, mix the dark rye flour, salt, olives and sundried tomatoes together and set aside. This is the dry mixture.

3 Add the dry mixture to the bubbling pre-ferment, add the hot water and mix thoroughly with a wooden spoon.

4 Transfer the dough to the prepared sandwich pan.

5 Sprinkle some extra dark rye flour on top for decoration. Slash the loaf with a sharp serrated knife or a lamé with a design of your own choice.

6 Allow to rise for 1–2 hours. Cover with a shower cap or a small mixing bowl if a skin starts to form. You will know when the dough is ready because cracks and little air holes will appear on the floured surface.

7 Preheat the oven to 250°C (500°F) Gas 9. Place a deep roasting tray at the bottom of the oven.

8 Place the loaf in the preheated oven. Pour a cup of water into the hot roasting tray and lower the temperature to 220°C (425°F) Gas 7.

9 Bake for 30–40 minutes until golden brown.

10 Turn the loaf out of the loaf pan and tap it on the bottom. If you hear a hollow sound, it is ready. If the loaf is still soft, return it to the oven for a further 10–15 minutes.

11 Allow the loaf to cool on a wire rack.

Prune and pepper rye sourdough

The pink peppercorns give this bread a nice gentle heat, particularly when mixed with the rich sweetness from the prunes.

TIME PLANNER

Making the pre-ferment **8 hours**

Making and shaping the dough **15 minutes**

Final proofing **1–2 hours**

Resting in the fridge **30 minutes**

Baking **30–40 minutes**

Cooling **30 minutes**

INGREDIENTS

200 g/1½ cups dark rye flour

6 g/1 teaspoon salt

200 g/1½ cups dried, stoned/pitted prunes, chopped into small pieces

10 g/2 teaspoons whole pink peppercorns, lightly crushed

200 g/200 ml/¾ cup hot water (just boiled)

porridge/rolled oats, for coating

For the pre-ferment

200 g/1½ cups dark rye flour

150 g/5½ oz. rye sourdough starter (see pages 16–17)

200 g/200 ml/¾ cup cold water

EQUIPMENT

1 x 800-g/1¾-lbs. round proofing/dough-rising basket

1 small peel, floured

Makes 1 x 800-g/1¾-lbs. loaf

1 To make the pre-ferment, add the dark rye flour, the rye sourdough starter and the cold water to a large mixing bowl and mix with a wooden spoon **(A)**. Leave to ferment for 8 hours or overnight, covered with a small mixing bowl acting as a lid.

2 The next day (or after 8 hours), in a small mixing bowl, mix the dark rye flour and salt together. This is the dry mixture.

3 Add the dry mixture to the bubbling pre-ferment **(B)**, add the hot water and mix thoroughly with a wooden spoon. **(C)** Add the prunes and then the peppercorns **(D)** and mix everything together **(E)**.

4 Coat the inside of the proofing/dough-rising basket with porridge/rolled oats. Using a plastic dough scraper, pick up the dough and coat it with the porridge/rolled oats and place it into the basket. Lightly flatten the top of the dough.

5 Allow to rise for 1–2 hours. Cover with a shower cap or with an upturned mixing bowl if a skin starts to form. You will know when it is ready because cracks and little air holes will appear on the surface. **(F)**

6 Place the dough in the fridge for 30 minutes to stabilize it.

7 Preheat the oven to 250°C (500°F) Gas 9. Place a deep roasting tray at the bottom of the oven and a baking sheet on the middle shelf.

8 Turn the dough out onto a floured peel. **(G)**

9 Slide the loaf onto the preheated baking sheet in the oven. Pour a cup of water into the hot roasting tray and lower the temperature to 220°C (425°F) Gas 7.

10 Bake for 30–40 minutes until golden brown.

11 Tap the loaf on the bottom. If you hear a hollow sound, it is ready. If not, return it to the oven for 10–15 minutes.

12 Remove the loaf from the baking sheet and allow it to cool on a wire rack.

A

B

Orange and coriander rye sourdough

This is a great German-style loaf packed full of so much flavour that it can be eaten on its own as well as spread with butter or marmalade (which goes perfectly with the hint of orange from the zest) or topped with other savoury delights. The coriander seeds give a lovely crunch.

TIME PLANNER

Making the pre-ferment **8 hours**

Making and shaping the dough **15 minutes**

Final proofing **1–2 hours**

Baking **30–40 minutes**

Cooling **30 minutes**

INGREDIENTS

200 g/1½ cups dark rye flour

2 teaspoons lightly crushed coriander seeds, plus extra for topping

zest of 1 orange or 2 small clementines or tangerines

6 g/1 teaspoon salt

150 g/150 ml/⅔ cup hot water (just boiled)

For the pre-ferment

150 g/1¼ cups dark rye flour

100 g/3½ oz. rye sourdough starter (see pages 16–17)

200 g/200 ml/¾ cup cold water

EQUIPMENT:

1 x 500-g/1-lb. loaf pan, greased with vegetable or sunflower oil

Makes 1 x 800-g/1¾-lbs. loaf

1 To make the pre-ferment, add the dark rye flour, the rye sourdough starter and the cold water to a large mixing bowl and mix with a wooden spoon. Leave to ferment for 8 hours or overnight, covered with a small mixing bowl acting as a lid.

2 The next day (or after 8 hours), prepare the dough. In a small mixing bowl, mix the dark rye flour, coriander seeds, orange (or tangerine or clementine) zest and salt together and set aside. This is the dry mixture.

3 Add the dry mixture to the bubbling pre-ferment, add the hot water and mix thoroughly with a wooden spoon.

4 Put the mixture into the greased loaf pan and shape using a plastic dough scraper.

5 Sprinkle some extra crushed coriander seeds on top for decoration.

6 Cover with the large mixing bowl or a shower cap and allow to rise for 1–2 hours in a warm place (see page 25). You will know when it is ready because cracks and little air holes will appear on the floured surface. Don't let it rise too much as it will overflow over the loaf pan.

7 Preheat the oven to 250°C (500°F) Gas 9 and place a deep roasting tray at the bottom of the oven.

8 Remove the large bowl or shower cap that has been covering the loaf and place the loaf pan in the preheated oven.

9 Pour a cup of water into the hot roasting tray and lower the temperature to 220°C (425°F) Gas 7.

10 Bake for 30–40 minutes until golden brown.

11 Tap the loaf on the bottom. If you hear a hollow sound, it is ready. If the loaf is still soft and you think it is not baked yet, return it to the oven for a further 10–15 minutes.

12 Turn the loaf out of the loaf pan and allow it to cool on a wire rack.

New York-style rye sourdough

This is my version of a New York rye bread with its distinctive caraway flavour. New York rye bread is usually rounded and slightly lighter than other rye breads. I've added white flour to make it a more typical dough. If you like, you can replace the caraway seeds with dill seeds.

TIME PLANNER

Making the dough **50 minutes**

Letting the dough rise **8–12 hours**

Knocking back and shaping the dough **10 minutes**

Final proofing **2–6 hours**

Resting in the fridge **30 minutes**

Baking **30–40 minutes**

Cooling **30 minutes**

INGREDIENTS

340 g/2½ cups white strong/bread flour, plus extra for dusting

200 g/1½ cups dark rye flour

5 g/1 teaspoon caraway seeds

11 g/2 teaspoons salt

27 g/1 oz. sourdough starter (see pages 16–17)

325 g/325 ml/1⅓ cups warm water (30–37°C/86–99°F)

EQUIPMENT

1 x 800-g/1¾-lbs. long proofing/dough-rising basket

Makes 1 x 800-g/1¾-lbs. loaf

1 In a small mixing bowl, mix the white flour, rye flour, caraway seeds and salt together thoroughly. This is the dry mixture.

2 Add the sourdough starter to a large mixing bowl. Add ¾ of the warm water and dissolve or break up the sourdough starter with your hands.

3 Add the dry mixture to the sourdough starter. Stir the mixture slowly with your hands until it comes together and there are no dry bits at the bottom of the bowl.

4 If the mixture doesn't come together and it seems a bit dry, add all of the remaining water. The dough should be slightly sticky. If it is still a bit dry, add more water and remember to record how much you used for next time.

5 Cover the mixture with the small mixing bowl that had the flour mixture in it. Leave to stand for 10 minutes.

6 Knead the mixture 10 times (see page 22).

7 Turn the ball of dough over in the bowl and make a finger mark in the dough (to indicate the first knead).

8 Cover with the small mixing bowl and leave the dough to rest for 10 minutes.

9 Repeat steps 6–8 another 3 times.

10 Cover the dough and leave it to rise overnight in a cool place (not in the fridge).

11 The next day, gently punch down to de-gas the dough.

12 Dust a long proofing/dough-rising basket with rye flour.

13 Remove the dough from the bowl, using a light sprinkling of flour so the dough does not stick. Shape the dough with your hands into a long loaf (see pages 28–29).

14 Coat the top of the dough with flour and place seam-up into the floured proofing/dough-rising basket.

15 Allow to proof for 2–6 hours or until the dough has nearly doubled in volume. Cover if a skin starts to form.

16 Place the dough in the fridge for 30 minutes to stabilize it.

17 Preheat the oven to 250°C (500°F) Gas 9. Place a deep roasting tray at the bottom of the oven and a baking sheet on the middle shelf.

18 Turn the dough out onto a floured peel.

19 Slash the loaf with a sharp serrated knife or a lamé with a design of your own choice.

20 Slide the loaf onto the preheated baking sheet in the oven. Pour a cup of water into the hot roasting tray and lower the temperature to 220°C (425°F) Gas 7.

21 Bake for 30–40 minutes until golden brown.

22 Tap the loaf on the bottom. If you hear a hollow sound, it is ready. If you are not sure, return it in the oven for a further 10 minutes.

23 Allow the loaf to cool on a wire rack.

FLAVOURED
SOURDOUGHS

A

B

C

D

Halloumi and mint sourdough

The salty springiness of halloumi is brought alive when it is fried in butter, giving it a delightful golden coating. Combining the halloumi with the nutty sesame seed coating and fresh mint makes for a lovely loaf.

TIME PLANNER

Frying the halloumi **5 minutes**

Making the dough **50 minutes**

Letting the dough rise
8–12 hours

Knocking back and shaping the dough **10 minutes**

Final proofing **2–6 hours**

Resting in the fridge **30 minutes**

Baking **30–40 minutes**

Cooling **30 minutes**

INGREDIENTS

100 g/3½ oz. halloumi cheese, sliced

knob/pat of butter

500 g/3½ cups white strong/bread flour

10 g/2 teaspoons salt

6 g/1 teaspoon chopped fresh mint

25 g/1 oz. sourdough starter (see pages 16–17)

300 g/300 ml/1¼ cups warm water (30–37°C/86–99°F)

sesame seeds, for coating

EQUIPMENT

1 x 800-g/1¾-lbs. long proofing/dough-rising basket

1 small peel, floured

Makes 1 x 800-g/1¾-lbs. loaf

1 Heat up some butter in a frying pan/skillet and when hot, add the halloumi. Fry for 2–3 minutes on each side until golden-brown and set aside **(A)**. Chop the halloumi into small pieces.

2 In a small mixing bowl, mix the flour, salt, chopped halloumi and mint together thoroughly. This is the dry mixture.

3 Add the sourdough starter to a large mixing bowl. Add ¾ of the warm water and dissolve or break up the sourdough starter with your hands. **(B)**

4 Add the dry mixture to the sourdough mixture **(C)**. Stir the mixture slowly with your hands or a wooden spoon until it comes together and there are no dry bits at the bottom of the bowl. **(D)**

5 If the mixture doesn't come together and it seems a bit dry, add some or all of the remaining water. The dough should be slightly sticky.

6 Cover the mixture with the small mixing bowl that had the flour mixture in it. Leave to stand for 10 minutes.

7 Knead the mixture. Start by squashing the dough with your knuckles and fingers

to flatten out any lumps. It should now look pancake-shaped.

8 Lift a portion of the dough up from the side and fold it into the middle and press with your knuckles.

9 Turn the bowl 90° clockwise, lift another portion of the dough up from the side and fold it into the middle and press with your knuckles.

10 Repeat steps 8–9 another 8 times (10 folds in total). If the dough starts to resist and tear, apply less pressure as you knead. If the dough becomes difficult to knead after kneading it 8 times, stop.

11 Turn the ball of dough over in the bowl and make a finger mark in the dough (to indicate the first knead). Cover with the bowl that had the flour in it. **(E)**

12 Leave the dough to rest for 10 minutes.

13 Repeat steps 8–12 another 3 times, making sure the mixture is covered between kneads and remembering to mark the dough to indicate the number of kneads you have done. **(F)**

14 Cover the dough and leave it to rise overnight in a cool place (not in the fridge, though). **(G: fully proofed dough)**

15 The next day, gently punch down to de-gas the dough.

16 Remove from the bowl, using a light sprinkling of flour so the dough does not stick. Shape the dough into a long loaf (see pages 28–29). **(H)**

17 Roll the loaf on a damp tea/dish towel, then coat it all over with sesame seeds. **(I)**

18 Place the loaf seam-up into the proofing/dough-rising basket and allow to proof for 2–6 hours or until the dough has nearly doubled in volume. Cover with a shower cap or with a mixing bowl if a skin starts to form. **(J) (K)**

19 Place the dough in the fridge for 30 minutes to stabilize it.

20 Preheat the oven to 250°C (500°F) Gas 9, place a deep roasting tray at the bottom of the oven and a baking sheet on the middle shelf.

21 Turn the dough out onto a floured peel.

22 Slash the loaf with a sharp serrated knife or a lamé with a design of your own choice. **(L)**

23 Slide the loaf onto the preheated baking sheet in the oven. Pour a cup of water into the hot roasting tray and lower the temperature to 200°C (400°F) Gas 6.

24 Bake for 30–40 minutes until golden brown, checking after 15 minutes as the sesame seed coating can burn quite quickly.

25 Tap the loaf on the bottom. If you hear a hollow sound, it is ready. If you are not sure, return it to the oven for a further 10 minutes.

26 Remove the loaf from the baking sheet and allow it to cool on a wire rack.

Potato, onion and dill sourdough

Dill seeds are not just for pickling – they've got a great flavour and partner perfectly with potato, especially if you have some leftover mash. This is one of my favourite loaves – it looks great when you cut into it.

TIME PLANNER

Making the dough **50 minutes**

Letting the dough rise
8–12 hours

Knocking back and shaping the dough **10 minutes**

Final proofing **2–6 hours**

Resting the dough in the fridge **30 minutes**

Baking **30–40 minutes**

Cooling **30 minutes**

INGREDIENTS

170 g/¾ cup mashed potato

85 g/⅔ cup red onion, thinly sliced

420 g/3 cups white strong/bread flour, plus extra for dusting

8 g/1½ teaspoons salt

6 g/1 teaspoon dill seeds

20 g/¾ oz. sourdough starter (see pages 16–17)

210 g/210 ml/¾ cup plus 2 tablespoons warm water (30–37°C/86–99°F)

EQUIPMENT

1 x 800-g/1¾-lbs. long proofing/dough-rising basket

1 small peel, floured

Makes 1 x 800-g/1¾-lbs. loaf

1 In a small mixing bowl, mix the mashed potato with the red onion.

2 In another small mixing bowl, mix the flour, salt and the dill seeds together thoroughly. This is the dry mixture.

3 Add the sourdough starter to a large mixing bowl. Add ¾ of the warm water and dissolve or break up the sourdough starter with your hands.

4 Add the dry mixture and the potato onion mixture to the sourdough mixture. Stir the mixture slowly with your hands until it comes together and there are no dry bits at the bottom of the bowl.

5 If the mixture doesn't come together and it seems a bit dry, add some or all of the remaining water. The dough should be slightly sticky.

6 Cover the mixture with the small mixing bowl that had the flour mixture in it. Leave to stand for 10 minutes.

7 Knead the mixture. Start by squashing the dough with your knuckles and fingers to flatten out any lumps. It should now look pancake-shaped.

8 Lift a portion of the dough up from the side and fold it into the middle and press with your knuckles.

9 Turn the bowl 90° clockwise, lift another portion of the dough up from the side and fold it into the middle and press with your knuckles.

10 Repeat steps 8–9 another 8 times (10 folds in total). If the dough starts to resist and starts to tear, apply less pressure as you knead. Also, if you can only knead it 8 times and it starts to resist, making it difficult to knead, stop.

11 Turn the ball of dough over in the bowl and make a finger mark in the dough (to indicate the first knead), and cover with the bowl that had the flour in it.

12 Leave the dough to rest for 10 minutes.

13 Repeat steps 8–12 another 3 times, making sure the mixture is covered between kneads and remembering to mark the dough to indicate the number of kneads you have done.

14 You are looking for a smooth, elastic dough. If you think the dough is not kneaded enough, repeat steps 8–10 another time.

15 Cover the dough and leave it to rise overnight in a cool place (but not in the fridge, though). If the dough is not covered, a skin will form and this will affect the end result. **(A)**

16 The next day, gently punch down to de-gas the dough.

17 Remove from the bowl, using a light sprinkling of flour so the dough does not stick. Shape the dough into a long loaf (see pages 28–29). Coat the top with flour and place seam-up into a floured long proofing/dough-rising basket. **(B)**

A

B

18 Allow to proof for 2–6 hours or until the dough has nearly doubled in volume. Cover with a shower cap or with an upturned mixing bowl if a skin starts to form.

19 Place the dough in the fridge for 30 minutes to stabilize it.

20 Preheat the oven to 250°C (500°F) Gas 9. Place a deep roasting tray at the bottom of the oven and a baking sheet on the middle shelf.

21 Turn the dough out onto a floured peel.

22 Slash the loaf with a sharp serrated knife or a lamé with a design of your own choice. **(C)**

23 Slide the loaf onto the preheated baking sheet in the oven. Pour a cup of water into the hot roasting tray and lower the temperature to 220°C (425°F) Gas 7.

24 Bake for 30–40 minutes until golden brown.

25 Tap the loaf on the bottom. If you hear a hollow sound, the loaf is ready. If you are not sure, return it to the oven for a further 10 minutes.

26 Remove the loaf from the baking sheet and allow it to cool on a wire rack.

Note: If you are using leftover mashed potato that already contains salt, you might want to lower the salt a little.

Parsnip and thyme sourdough

Certainly not just for Christmas, the humble parsnip gives a lovely earthy sweetness to a sourdough loaf. Try dipping slices of this bread into a steaming hot bowl of soup.

TIME PLANNER

Making the dough 50 minutes

Letting the dough rise 8–12 hours

Knocking back and shaping the dough 10 minutes

Final proofing 2–6 hours

Resting the dough in the fridge 30 minutes

Baking 30–40 minutes

Cooling 30 minutes

INGREDIENTS

460 g/3 cups plus 3 tablespoons white strong/bread flour, plus extra for dusting

10 g/2 teaspoons salt

180 g/1⅓ cups coarsely grated parsnip

2 g/½ teaspoon fresh thyme

25 g/1 oz. sourdough starter (see pages 16–17)

230 g/230 ml/1 scant cup warm water (30–37°C/86–99°F)

EQUIPMENT

1 x 800-g/1¾-lbs. long proofing/dough-rising basket

1 small peel, floured

Makes 1 x 800-g/1¾-lbs. loaf

1 In a small mixing bowl, mix the flour, salt, parsnip and thyme together thoroughly and set aside. This is the dry mixture.

2 Add the sourdough starter to a large mixing bowl. Add ¾ of the warm water and dissolve or break up the sourdough starter with your hands or wait for it to dissolve.

3 Add the dry mixture. Stir the mixture slowly with your hands until it comes together and there are no dry bits at the bottom of the bowl.

4 If the mixture doesn't come together and it seems a bit dry, add some or all of the remaining water (note that it's best to keep the dough slightly stiff as the parsnip will add more moisture to the dough).

5 Cover the mixture with the small mixing bowl that had the flour mixture in it. Leave to stand for 10 minutes.

6 Knead the mixture 10 times.

7 Turn the ball of dough over in the bowl and make a finger mark in the dough (to indicate the first knead).

8 Cover with the small mixing bowl and leave the dough to rest for 10 minutes.

9 Repeat steps 6–8 another 3 times, making sure the mixture is covered between kneads and remembering to mark the dough to indicate the number of kneads done.

10 Cover the dough and leave it to rise overnight in a cool place (not in the fridge, though).

11 The next day, gently punch down to de-gas the dough.

12 Remove from the bowl, using a light sprinkling of flour so the dough does not stick. Shape the dough into a long loaf (see pages 28–29). Coat the top with flour and place the loaf seam-up into a floured long proofing/dough-rising basket.

13 Allow to proof for 2–6 hours or until the dough has nearly doubled in volume. Cover with a shower cap or with a mixing bowl if a skin starts to form.

14 Place the dough in the fridge for 30 minutes to stabilize it.

15 Preheat the oven to 250°C (500°F) Gas 9. Place a deep roasting tray at the bottom of the oven and a baking sheet on the middle shelf.

16 Turn the dough out onto a floured peel.

17 Slash the loaf with a sharp serrated knife or a lamé with a design of your choice.

18 Slide the loaf onto the preheated baking sheet in the oven. Pour a cup of water into the hot roasting tray and lower the temperature to 220°C (425°F) Gas 7.

19 Bake for 30–40 minutes until golden brown.

20 Tap the loaf on the bottom. If you hear a hollow sound, it is ready. If you are not sure, return it to the oven for a further 10 minutes.

21 Remove the loaf from the baking sheet and allow it to cool on a wire rack.

Rosemary and raisin sourdough

Rosemary and raisin is a popular Italian combination, and this fruity, moist bread pairs equally well with savoury and sweet foods. Ordinary raisins are fine to use as they will plump up nicely overnight. You can try using sultanas/golden raisins too, as an alternative.

TIME PLANNER (see page 73)

INGREDIENTS

300 g/2¼ cups white strong/bread flour, plus extra for dusting

120 g/1 scant cup wholemeal/wholewheat flour

8 g/1½ teaspoons salt

120 g/1 scant cup raisins

16 g/1 tablespoon chopped fresh rosemary

20 g/¾ oz. sourdough starter (see pages 16–17)

320 g/320 ml/1⅓ cups warm water (30–37°C/86–99°F)

EQUIPMENT

1 x 800-g/1¾-lbs. round proofing basket/dough-rising basket

1 small peel, floured

Makes 1 x 800-g/1¾-lbs. loaf

1 In a small mixing bowl, mix the flour, salt, raisins and rosemary together thoroughly and set aside. This is the dry mixture.

2 Add the sourdough starter and ¾ of the warm water to a large mixing bowl. Dissolve or break up the sourdough starter with your hands.

3 Add the dry mixture. Stir the mixture slowly with your hands until it comes together and there are no dry bits at the bottom of the bowl.

4 If the mixture doesn't come together and it seems a bit dry, add some or all of the remaining water. The dough should be slightly sticky.

5 Cover the mixture with the small mixing bowl. Leave to stand for 10 minutes.

6 Knead the mixture 10 times.

7 Turn the ball of dough over in the bowl and make a finger mark in the dough (to indicate the first knead).

8 Cover with the small mixing bowl and leave the dough to rest for 10 minutes.

9 Repeat steps 6–8 another 3 times, making sure the mixture is covered between kneads and remembering to mark the dough to indicate the number of kneads done.

10 Cover the dough and leave it to rise overnight in a cool place (not in the fridge, though).

11 The next day, gently punch down to de-gas the dough.

12 Remove from the bowl, using a light sprinkling of flour so the dough does not stick. Shape the dough into a ball (see pages 24–25).

13 Coat the proofing/dough-rising basket and the top of the loaf with flour. Place the dough seam-up into the basket. **(A)**

14 Allow to proof for 2–6 hours or until the dough has nearly doubled in volume. Cover with a shower cap or with an upturned mixing bowl if a skin starts to form.

15 Place the dough in the fridge for 30 minutes to stabilize it.

16 Preheat the oven to 250°C (500°F) Gas 9 and place a deep roasting tray at the bottom of the oven and a baking sheet on the middle shelf.

17 Turn the dough out onto a floured peel.

18 Slash the loaf with a sharp serrated knife or a lamé with a design of your own choice. **(B)**

19 Slide the loaf onto the preheated baking sheet and into the oven. Pour a cup of water into the hot roasting tray and lower the temperature to 220°C (425°F) Gas 7.

20 Bake for 30–40 minutes until golden brown.

21 Tap the loaf on the bottom. If you hear a hollow sound, it is ready. If you are not sure, return it to the oven for a further 10 minutes.

22 Remove the loaf from the baking sheet and allow it to cool on a wire rack.

Date and walnut sourdough

Date and walnut is such a rich, aromatic combination. This bread works really well with an aged cheese, such as manchego or Pecorino Romano.

TIME PLANNER

Making the dough **50 minutes**

Letting the dough rise **8–12 hours**

Knocking back and shaping the dough **10 minutes**

Final proofing **2–6 hours**

Resting in the fridge **30 minutes**

Baking **30–40 minutes**

Cooling **30 minutes**

INGREDIENTS

290 g/scant 2½ cups white strong/bread flour, plus extra for dusting

150 g/1 generous cup wholemeal/wholewheat flour

8 g/1½ teaspoons salt

80 g/⅔ cup chopped dates

60 g/½ cup chopped walnuts

20 g/¾ oz. sourdough starter (see pages 16–17)

300 g/300 ml/1¼ cups warm water (30–37°C/86–99°F)

EQUIPMENT:

1 x 800-g/1¾-lbs. long proofing/dough-rising basket

1 small peel, floured

Makes 1 x 800-g/1¾-lbs. loaf

1 In a small mixing bowl, mix the white and wholemeal/wholewheat flours, salt, dates and walnuts together thoroughly. This is the dry mixture.

2 Add the sourdough starter to a large mixing bowl. Add ¾ of the warm water and dissolve or break up the sourdough starter with your hands.

3 Add the dry mixture. Stir the mixture slowly with your hands until it comes together and there are no dry bits at the bottom of the bowl.

4 If the mixture doesn't come together and it seems a bit dry, add some or all of the remaining water. The dough should be slightly sticky.

5 Cover the mixture with the small mixing bowl that had the flour mixture in it. Leave to stand for 10 minutes.

6 Knead the mixture 10 times.

7 Turn the ball of dough over in the bowl and make a finger mark in the dough (to indicate the first knead).

8 Cover with the small mixing bowl and leave the dough to rest for 10 minutes.

9 Repeat steps 6–8 another 3 times, making sure the mixture is covered between kneads and remembering to mark the dough to indicate the number of kneads you have done.

10 Cover the dough and leave it to rise overnight in a cool place (not in the fridge, though).

11 The next day, gently punch down to de-gas the dough.

12 Dust a long proofing/dough-rising basket liberally with flour.

13 Remove from the bowl, using a light sprinkling of flour so the dough does not stick. Shape the dough into a long loaf (see pages 28–29). Coat the top with flour and place the loaf seam-up into the proofing/dough-rising basket.

14 Place the loaf seam-up into the proofing/dough-rising basket.

15 Allow to proof for 2–6 hours or until the dough has nearly doubled in volume. Cover if a skin starts to form.

16 Place the dough in the fridge for 30 minutes to stabilize it.

17 Preheat the oven to 250°C (500°F) Gas 9 and place a deep roasting tray at the bottom of the oven and a baking sheet on the middle shelf.

18 Turn the dough out onto a floured peel.

19 Slash the loaf with a sharp serrated knife or a lamé with a design of your own choice.

20 Slide the loaf onto the preheated baking sheet in the oven. Pour a cup of water into the hot roasting tray and lower the temperature to 220°C (425°F) Gas 7.

21 Bake for 30–40 minutes until golden brown.

22 Tap the loaf on the bottom. If you hear a hollow sound, it is ready. If you are not sure, return it to the oven for a further 10 minutes.

23 Allow the loaf to cool on a wire rack.

Apple and cinnamon sourdough

The lovely apple and cinnamon mixture and the unusual shape makes this feel quite festive. It's a wonderful way to use up old apples!

TIME PLANNER

Making the dried apple **1 hour**

Making the dough **50 minutes**

Letting the dough rise **8–12 hours**

Knocking back and shaping the dough **10 minutes**

Final proofing **2–6 hours**

Resting in the fridge **30 minutes**

Baking **30–40 minutes**

Cooling **30 minutes**

INGREDIENTS

3 sweet apples

450 g/3 cups plus 2 tablespoons white strong/bread flour, plus extra for topping the loaf

7 g/1¼ teaspoons salt

4 g/1 teaspoon ground cinnamon

25 g/1 oz. sourdough starter (see pages 16–17)

300 g/300 ml/2¼ cups warm water (30–37°C/86–99°F)

45 g/¼ cup coarsely grated sweet apple

EQUIPMENT

1 baking sheet, lined with baking parchment

1 x 800-g/1¾-lbs. round proofing/dough-rising basket, with a centre insert, coated with flour

1 small peel, floured

Makes 1 x 800-g/1¾-lbs. loaf

1 Cut the apples into slices about 2 mm/ ¹⁄₁₆ inches thick and place on a baking sheet lined with baking parchment. Bake at 150°C (300°F) Gas 2 for 30 minutes, then lower the temperature to 100°C (210°F) Gas ¼ for 30 minutes. Bake until leathery, but not too dried out. **(A)**

2 In a small mixing bowl mix the flour, salt, dried apple (you'll need approx. 80 g/3 oz.) and cinnamon thoroughly with a wooden spoon. This is the dry mixture.

3 Add the sourdough starter to a large mixing bowl. Add ¾ of the warm water and dissolve or break the sourdough starter up with your hands.

4 Add the grated apple to the sourdough.

5 Add the dry mixture. Stir the mixture with your hands until it comes together. Add some of the remaining water if needed.

6 Cover the mixture with the small mixing bowl. Leave to stand for 10 minutes.

7 Knead the mixture 10 times (page 22).

8 Turn the ball of dough over in the bowl and make a finger mark in the dough. Cover and leave to rest for 10 minutes.

9 Repeat steps 7–8 another 3 times. Cover the dough and leave it to rise overnight in a cool place (not in the fridge).

10 The next day, gently punch down to de-gas the dough.

11 Remove the dough, using a sprinkling of flour. Shape the dough into a ball (see pages 24–25) and make a hole in the centre using your elbow and fingers. **(B) (C)**

12 Sprinkle the top of the dough with extra flour and place seam-up into the floured proofing/dough-rising basket. **(D)**

13 Proof for 2–6 hours or until the dough has doubled in volume. Cover if a skin forms.

14 Place the dough in the fridge for 30 minutes to stabilize it.

15 Preheat the oven to 250°C (500°F) Gas 9. Place a roasting tray at the bottom and a baking sheet on the middle shelf.

16 Turn the dough out onto a floured peel.

17 Slash the loaf with a sharp serrated knife or a lamé with your own design.

18 Slide the loaf onto the preheated baking sheet in the oven. Pour a cup of water into the hot roasting tray and lower the temperature to 220°C (425°F) Gas 7.

19 Bake for 30–40 minutes until golden brown. Allow to cool on a wire rack.

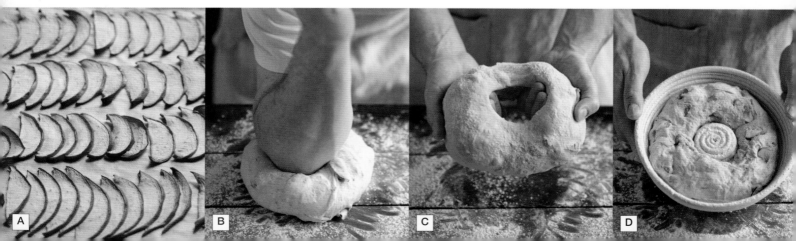

A B C D

Carrot and ginger sourdough

The trick with this bread is to grate the carrots coarsely so that they retain their colour and don't melt into the dough when the bread is baked. The result is a fantastic orange polka-dot finish to the crumb.

TIME PLANNER

Making the dough **50 minutes**

Letting the dough rise **1 hour**

Knocking back and shaping the dough **10 minutes**

Final proofing **2–6 hours**

Resting the dough in the fridge **30 minutes**

Baking **30–40 minutes**

Cooling **30 minutes**

INGREDIENTS

350 g/2⅔ cups white strong/bread flour, plus extra for topping the loaf

4 g/1 teaspoon salt

175 g/1 cup plus 3 tablespoons coarsely grated carrot

20 g/4 teaspoons chopped crystallized ginger

6 g/1 teaspoon ground cinnamon

80 g/2¾ oz. sourdough starter (see pages 16–17)

175 g/175 ml/¾ cup warm water (30–37°C/86–99°F)

70 g/⅓ cup brown sugar

20 g/20 ml/2 tablespoons sunflower oil

EQUIPMENT

1 x 800-g/1¾-lbs. loaf pan, greased with vegetable or sunflower oil

Makes 1 x 800-g/1¾-lbs. loaf

1 In a small mixing bowl, mix the flour and salt together thoroughly. Set aside. This is the dry mixture.

2 In another small mixing bowl, mix the carrot, crystallized ginger and ground cinnamon and set aside.

3 Add the sourdough starter to a large mixing bowl. Add ¾ of the warm water and dissolve or break up the sourdough starter with your hands.

4 Add the brown sugar to the sourdough starter and mix together until the sugar has dissolved.

5 Add the dry mixture and the carrot mixture, and stir the mixture slowly with your hands until it comes together and there are no dry bits at the bottom of the bowl.

6 If the mixture doesn't come together and it seems a bit dry, add some of the remaining water. The dough should be slightly sticky. If it still seems dry, add some more water and remember how much you used for next time.

7 Add the sunflower oil to another large mixing bowl, then transfer the dough into it. Cover with the small mixing bowl and leave to stand for 10 minutes.

8 Knead the mixture 10 times (page 22).

9 Turn the ball of dough over in the bowl and make a finger mark in the dough (to indicate the first knead).

10 Cover with the small mixing bowl and leave the dough to rest for 10 minutes.

11 Repeat steps 8–10 another 3 times. Remember to cover the mixture between kneads and mark the dough to indicate the amount of kneads done.

12 Cover the dough and leave it to rise for 1 hour in a cool place (not in the fridge, though).

13 After 1 hour, gently punch down to de-gas the dough.

14 Shape the dough with your hands until it is roughly the length and width of the loaf pan. Place seam-down in the greased loaf pan and coat the top with a light sprinkling of flour.

15 Cover with a shower cap or with a mixing bowl. Allow to proof for 2–6 hours or until the dough has nearly doubled in volume.

16 Preheat the oven to 250°C (500°F) Gas 9 and place a deep roasting tray at the bottom of the oven.

17 Place the loaf in the preheated oven. Pour a cup of water into the hot roasting tray and lower the temperature to 200°C (400°F) Gas 6.

18 Bake for 30–40 minutes until golden brown.

19 Tap the loaf on the bottom. If you hear a hollow sound, it is ready. If you are not sure, return it to the oven for a further 10 minutes.

20 Turn the loaf out of the loaf pan and allow it to cool on a wire rack.

CULTURED SOURDOUGHS

What is kefir?

Kefir is a fermented milk drink that originated in eastern Europe and parts of southwest Asia. It is similar to a drinking yogurt and has a tart and refreshing flavour. Kefir is practically lactose-free and easier to digest than unfermented milk. It has become popular in western Europe and the US on account of its widely touted digestive health benefits, on top of the fact it contains many valuable vitamins and minerals. Kefir is increasingly available in supermarkets but it tastes even better when you make your own.

How is kefir made?

Kefir is made by adding kefir grains – live cultures of yeast and lactic acid bacteria which clump together with milk proteins and complex sugars – to milk. Any type of milk can be used, including cow's milk, goat's milk, coconut milk, rice milk or soy milk. Kefir grains look like gelatinous grains of rice and form cauliflower-like structures when they group together. Kefir grains feed on the lactose in milk. The grains work a little bit like a sourdough starter in that they kick-start the fermentation process, but unlike a sourdough starter, they are removed after they have multiplied and fermented the milk sugars.

INGREDIENTS

1 tablespoon kefir grains

240 g/240 ml/1 cup cow's milk, goat's milk or any other milk

EQUIPMENT

1 x 720-ml/24-fl. oz. glass jar

1 x plastic or nylon mesh sieve/strainer

1 x paper towel or muslin/cheesecloth

1 x rubber band

Makes 240 ml/1 cup

In the glass jar, add the kefir grains to the milk. Cover with a paper towel or a clean muslin/cheesecloth and let rest in a pantry or on a work surface for 18–24 hours. Strain the kefir from the grains and it's ready to use. Keep the strained grains in the fridge ready to add to another batch of milk.

Kefir or yogurt sourdough

TIME PLANNER

Making the pre-ferment **8 hours**

Making the dough **50 minutes**

Letting the dough rise **1 hour**

Knocking back and shaping the dough **10 minutes**

Final proofing **2–6 hours**

Resting in the fridge **30 minutes**

Baking **30–40 minutes**

Cooling **30 minutes**

INGREDIENTS

180 g/1¼ cups white strong/bread flour, plus extra for dusting

8 g/1½ teaspoons salt

zest of 1 lemon

90 g/3 oz. kefir or a mixture of 50% yogurt and 50% milk, at room temperature

For the pre-ferment

180 g/1¼ cups white strong/bread flour

90 g/¾ cup light rye flour or sifted dark rye flour

80 g/2¾ oz. sourdough starter (see pages 16–17)

270 g/10 oz. kefir or pouring yogurt or a mixture of 50% set yogurt and 50% milk, at room temperature

EQUIPMENT

1 x 800-g/1¾-lbs. round proofing/ dough-rising basket

1 small peel, floured

Makes 1 x 800-g/1¾-lbs. loaf

You can either use pre-bought kefir for this recipe or make your own using the instructions on the opposite page. Alternatively, a mixture of set yogurt and milk will work just as well. The sourness of the yogurt or kefir brings out the lemon in the recipe and makes for an intense flavour.

1 First make the pre-ferment. In a small mixing bowl, mix the strong/bread flour and light rye or dark rye flour together and set aside. In a large mixing bowl, dissolve or break up the sourdough starter in the kefir or yogurt and milk mixture, then add the flour mixture and mix together to form a paste consistency. Scrape round the edges and cover with an upturned small mixing bowl. Leave to ferment in a warm place for 8 hours or overnight. **(A) (B)**

2 After 8 hours, in another small mixing bowl, mix the strong/bread flour, salt and lemon zest together thoroughly and set aside. This is the dry mixture.

3 The pre-ferment should be bubbling and emit a lactic smell. Mix the dry mixture into the pre-ferment, add ¾ of the kefir or yogurt and milk mixture and mix until it comes together.

4 If the mixture seems a bit dry, add a little or all of the remaining kefir or yogurt and milk mixture.

5 Cover the mixture with an upturned small mixing bowl.

6 Leave to stand for 10 minutes.

7 Knead the mixture. Start by squashing the dough with your knuckles and fingers to flatten out any lumps. It should now look pancake-shaped.

8 Lift a portion of the dough up from the side and fold it into the middle and press with your knuckles.

9 Turn the bowl 90° clockwise and lift another portion of the dough up from the side and fold it into the middle and press with your knuckles.

10 Repeat steps 8–9 another 8 times, (10 folds in total).

11 Turn the ball of dough over in the bowl and make a finger mark in the dough (to indicate the first knead). Cover with a small mixing bowl.

12 Leave to rest for 10 minutes.

13 Repeat steps 8–12 another 3 times, remembering to mark the dough to indicate the amount of kneads you have done **(C)**. You are looking for smooth, elastic dough. If you think the dough is not kneaded enough, repeat steps 9–13 another time.

14 Cover and leave to rise for 1 hour in a warm place.

15 After 1 hour, gently punch down to de-gas the dough.

16 Remove from the bowl and transfer the dough to a work surface that has been lightly sprinkled with white flour so the dough does not stick.

17 To shape the ball of dough into a rounded loaf, first, flatten the dough slightly with your palm.

18 Take a corner of the dough and fold it right over to the opposite side then turn the dough 90° clockwise.

19 Repeat the previous step 4–5 more times until the dough is a roundish shape. Then turn the dough over and tuck in the underneath of the dough with your fingers as you rotate the dough clockwise until you've formed a rounded ball. **(D)**

20 Coat the proofing/dough-rising basket and the top of the dough with flour and place the dough seam-up into the basket. **(E)**

21 Allow to proof for 2–6 hours or until the dough has nearly doubled in volume **(F)**. Cover if a skin starts to form.

22 Place the dough in the fridge for 30 minutes to stabilize it.

23 Preheat the oven to 250°C (500°F) Gas 9 and place a deep roasting tray on the bottom of the oven and a baking sheet on the middle shelf.

24 Turn the dough out onto a floured peel.

25 Slash the loaf with a sharp serrated knife or a lamé with a design of your own choice. I've decorated it with a triangular pattern. **(G)**

26 Slide the loaf onto the preheated baking sheet in the oven. Pour a cup of water into the hot roasting tray and lower the temperature to 220°C (425°F) Gas 7.

27 Bake for 30–40 minutes until golden brown.

28 Tap the loaf on the bottom. If you hear a hollow sound, it is ready. If you are not sure, return it to the oven for a further 10 minutes.

29 Remove the loaf from the baking sheet and allow it to cool on a wire rack.

INGREDIENTS

120 g/1 scant cup white strong/bread flour, plus extra for dusting

180 g/1⅓ cups wholemeal/wholewheat flour

36 g/1¼ oz. pale malt (Maris Otter), crushed

36 g/1¼ oz. crystal malt, crushed

12 g/½ oz. dark malt (chocolate malt), crushed

10 g/2 teaspoons salt

270 g/270 ml/1 cup plus 2 tablespoons warm water (30–37°C/86–99°F)

porridge/rolled oats, for coating

For building up the beer barm

15 g/½ oz. fresh beer barm

150 g/150 ml/⅔ cup beer (German wheat beer works well)

150 g/1 generous cup strong/bread flour or wholemeal/wholewheat flour

EQUIPMENT

1 x 800-g/1¾-lbs. long proofing/dough-rising basket

1 small peel, floured

Makes 1 x 800-g/1¾-lbs. loaf

Malted beer barm loaf

Beer and bread have a long history, particularly in Britain. Beer barm is the foam that appears on the top of the fermenting liquid during brewing. For centuries this barm was used as yeast to leaven bread, creating a slightly sweet-tasting loaf. Fresh beer barm is available from your local brewery and the three main grains in this recipe are all available online.

1 The day before you want to bake the bread, build up the beer barm in a small mixing bowl. Dissolve the fresh beer barm into the beer, then add the strong/bread flour or wholemeal/wholewheat flour. Cover and leave to ferment for 8 hours or overnight. If you find it starts to bubble after 4 hours, place it in the fridge, making sure it is covered.

2 In a small mixing bowl, mix the flours, the three kinds of malt and the salt together thoroughly and set aside. This is the dry mixture. **(A)**

3 Take 200 g/7 oz. beer barm from the mixture you have built up (reserve the rest for next time). **(B)**

4 Add the beer barm to a large mixing bowl. Add ¾ of the warm water and break up the beer barm with your hands. **(C)**

5 Add the dry mixture **(D)**. Stir the mixture slowly with your hands or a wooden spoon until it comes together and there are no dry bits at the bottom of the bowl. **(E)**

6 If the mixture doesn't come together and it seems a bit dry, add some of the remaining water. The dough should be slightly sticky.

7 Cover the mixture with the small mixing bowl that had the flour mixture in it. Leave to stand for 10 minutes.

8 Knead the mixture 10 times (see page 22).

9 Turn the ball of dough over in the bowl and make a finger mark in the dough (to indicate the first knead).

10 Cover with the small mixing bowl and leave the dough to rest for 10 minutes. **(F)**

A   B   C

11 Repeat steps 8–10 another 3 times, making sure the mixture is covered between kneads and remembering to mark the dough to indicate the amount of kneads you have done. If the dough starts to resist and starts to tear, apply less pressure as you knead. If the dough becomes difficult to knead after kneading it 8 times, stop.

12 After you have done 4 kneads with a 10 minute break between them, cover and leave the dough to rise for 1 hour in a warm place.

13 After 1 hour, gently punch down to de-gas your dough.

14 Remove from the bowl, using a light sprinkling of flour so the dough does not stick. Shape the dough into a ball (see pages 24–25) and leave it to rest before rolling it into a long shape (see pages 28–29). **(G) (H) (I)**

15 Roll the top of the loaf on a damp tea/dish towel, then coat the top all over with porridge/rolled oats **(J)**. Place the dough seam-up into a proofing/dough-rising basket that has been coated with porridge/rolled oats. **(K) (L)**

16 Allow to proof for 2–4 hours or until the dough has nearly doubled in volume. Cover if a skin starts to form.

17 Place the dough in the fridge for 30 minutes to stabilize it so it does not spread like a pancake on the peel.

18 Preheat the oven to 250°C (500°F) Gas 9. Place a deep roasting tray at the bottom of the oven and a baking sheet on the middle shelf.

19 Turn the dough out onto a floured peel.

20 Slash the top of the loaf with a sharp serrated knife or a lamé with a design of your own choice. Alternatively, leave it plain.

21 Slide the loaf onto the preheated baking sheet in the oven. Pour a cup of water into the hot roasting tray and lower the temperature to 220°C (425°F) Gas 7.

22 Bake for 30–40 minutes until golden brown.

23 Tap the loaf on the bottom. If you hear a hollow sound, it is ready. If you are not sure, return it to the oven for a further 10 minutes.

24 Remove the loaf from the baking sheet and allow it to cool on a wire rack.

Stottie beer barm loaf

Originating in northeast England, where it is known as 'stottie cake', this is a traditional bread made with lard rather than butter. Uniquely in this book, it is turned over halfway through baking.

INGREDIENTS

450 g/3 cups plus 2 tablespoons white strong/bread flour

9 g/2 teaspoons salt

50 g/½ stick butter, chopped into small pieces

240 g/240 ml/1 cup warm water (30–37°C/86–99°F)

semolina, for topping

For building up the beer barm

10 g/⅓ oz. fresh beer barm

100 g/100 ml/7 tablespoons warm water (30–37°C/86–99°F)

100 g/¾ cup plain/all-purpose flour

EQUIPMENT

1 baking sheet lined with baking parchment

1 small peel, floured

Makes 1 x 800-g/1¾-lbs. loaf

1 The day before, build up the beer barm (follow step 1 on page 89).

2 In a small mixing bowl, mix the flour, salt and butter together thoroughly and set aside. This is the dry mixture.

3 Add 125 g/4½ oz. of built-up beer barm to a large mixing bowl. Add ¾ of the warm water and break up the beer barm with your hands.

4 Add the dry mixture to the beer barm. Stir the mixture slowly with your hands until it comes together. Add the remaining water if needed.

5 Cover the mixture with the small mixing bowl. Leave to stand for 10 minutes.

6 Knead the mixture 10 times (see page 22).

7 Turn the ball of dough over in the bowl and make a finger mark in the dough.

8 Cover with the small mixing bowl and leave the dough to rest for 10 minutes.

9 Repeat steps 6–8 another 3 times.

10 Cover and leave the dough to rise overnight in a cool place (not in the fridge).

11 Punch down to de-gas the dough.

12 Remove from the bowl, using a light sprinkling of flour. Shape the dough into a ball (see pages 24–25).

13 Sprinkle semolina on the prepared baking sheet. Gently flatten the dough with a rolling pin or with your hands **(A)**. Place the dough on the baking sheet. Coat the top with semolina and make a hole in the middle with your finger. **(B)**

14 Allow to proof for 30–60 minutes or until the dough has nearly doubled in volume and cracks form on the surface.

15 Preheat the oven to 250°C (500°F) Gas 9 and place a deep roasting tray at the bottom of the oven and a baking sheet on the middle shelf.

16 Slide the loaf (on the parchment paper) onto a peel. Make the hole in the dough a bit bigger. Slide the loaf onto the preheated baking sheet in the oven.

17 Pour a cup of water into the hot roasting tray and lower the temperature to 220°C (425°F) Gas 7.

18 Bake for 10–15 minutes until it starts to colour. Remove the baking sheet from the oven **(C)**. Turn the loaf over **(D)** and bake for 10–15 minutes more. Cool on a wire rack.

A   B   C   D

Country beer barm loaf

This beer barm sourdough includes a mixture of white, wholemeal/wholewheat and rye flours. It's a variation of pain de campagne, which would have originally featured stone-ground flour and beer barm as the rising agent. Feel free to experiment with the decorative touches.

TIME PLANNER

Building up the beer barm **8 hours**

Making the dough **50 minutes**

Letting the dough rise **1 hour**

Knocking back and shaping the dough **10 minutes**

Final proofing **2–4 hours**

Resting in the fridge **30 minutes**

Baking **30–40 minutes**

Cooling **30 minutes**

INGREDIENTS

250 g/2 scant cups white strong/bread flour, plus extra for dusting

100 g/¾ cup wholemeal/wholewheat flour

50 g/scant ½ cup dark rye flour

8 g/1½ teaspoons salt

280 g/280 ml/1 cup plus 3 tablespoons warm water (30–37°C/86–99°F)

For building up the beer barm

10 g/⅓ oz. fresh beer barm

100 g/100 ml/7 tablespoons warm water (30–37°C/86–99°F)

100 g/¾ cup white strong/bread flour

EQUIPMENT

1 x 800-g/1¾-lbs. round proofing/dough-rising basket

1 small peel, floured

Makes 1 x 800-g/1¾-lbs. loaf

---

1 The day before you want to bake the bread, build up the beer barm in a small mixing bowl. Dissolve the fresh beer barm into the warm water, then add the flour. Cover and leave to ferment for 8 hours or overnight. If you find it starts to bubble after 4 hours, place it in the fridge, making sure it is covered. **(A)**

2 In a small mixing bowl, mix the flours and salt together thoroughly and set aside. This is the dry mixture.

3 Take 150 g/5½ oz. beer barm from the mixture you have built up and add it to a large mixing bowl. Add ¾ of the warm water and break up the beer barm with your hands. Reserve the rest for next time.

4 Add the dry mixture to the beer barm. Stir the mixture slowly with your hands until it comes together. If it doesn't, add some or all of the remaining water.

5 Cover the mixture with the small mixing bowl. Leave to stand for 10 minutes.

6 Knead the mixture 10 times (see page 22).

7 Turn the ball of dough over in the bowl and make a finger mark in the dough (to indicate the first knead).

8 Cover with the small mixing bowl and leave the dough to rest for 10 minutes.

9 Repeat steps 6–8 another 3 times.

10 Leave the dough to rise for 1 hour in a warm place and cover.

11 After 1 hour, gently punch down to de-gas the dough.

12 Remove from the bowl, using a light sprinkling of flour so the dough does not stick **(B)**. Shape the dough into a ball (see pages 24–25). **(C)**

13 Coat the proofing/dough-rising basket with flour. Coat the top of the dough with flour and place seam-up into the basket. **(D) (E) (F)**

14 Allow to proof for 2–4 hours or until the dough has nearly doubled in volume. Cover with a shower cap or with a mixing bowl if a skin starts to form.

15 Place the dough in the fridge for 30 minutes to stabilize it.

16 Preheat the oven to 250°C (500°F) Gas 9. Place a deep roasting tray at the bottom of the oven and a baking sheet on the middle shelf.

17 Turn the dough out onto a floured peel.

18 Slash the loaf with a sharp serrated knife or a lamé with a design of your own choice. **(G)**

19 Slide the loaf onto the preheated baking sheet in the oven. Pour a cup of water into the hot roasting tray and lower the temperature to 220°C (425°F) Gas 7.

20 Bake for 30–40 minutes until golden brown.

21 Tap the loaf on the bottom. If you hear a hollow sound, it is ready. If you are not sure, return it to the oven for a further 10 minutes.

22 Remove the loaf from the baking sheet and allow it to cool on a wire rack.

GLUTEN-FREE
SOURDOUGHS

Plain gluten-free sourdough

I've included two varieties for this bread: one with four flours, and one just using buckwheat flour. Bear in mind that the consistency of the dough will be more like a batter, it will not require kneading, and the mixture won't rise as much during proofing.

TIME PLANNER

Making the dough **10 minutes**

Letting the dough rise **8 hours**

Knocking back and shaping the dough **10 minutes**

Final proofing **2–6 hours**

Baking **35–40 minutes**

Cooling **30 minutes**

INGREDIENTS

350 g/2¾ cups plain gluten-free flour or 350 g/2¾ cups buckwheat flour

8 g/1½ teaspoons salt

20 g/¾ oz. gluten-free sourdough starter (see pages 16–17)

320 g/320 ml/1⅓ cups warm water (30–37°C/86–99°F)

OR

100 g/⅔ cup potato flour/potato starch

120 g/1 cup brown rice flour

80 g/⅔ cup buckwheat flour

50 g/3 tablespoons maize flour

8 g/1½ teaspoons salt

20 g/¾ oz. gluten-free sourdough starter (see pages 16–17)

320 g/320 ml/1⅓ cups warm water (30–37°C/86–99°F)

EQUIPMENT

1 x 500-g/1-lb. loaf pan, greased with vegetable or sunflower oil

Makes 1 x 500-g/1-lb. loaf

1 Add the flour(s) and salt to a small mixing bowl, mix them together thoroughly and set aside. This is the dry mixture. **(A)**

2 In the large mixing bowl, add the buckwheat sourdough starter and the warm water. Dissolve or break up the sourdough starter with your hands. **(B)**

3 Add the dry mixture to the buckwheat sourdough starter and mix together until it forms a soft mixture. **(C) (D)**

4 Cover the dough and leave it to rise overnight in a cool place (but not in the fridge). **(E)**

5 The next day **(F)**, deflate the dough by stirring it with a wooden spoon.

6 Transfer the dough into the greased loaf pan using a plastic dough scraper **(G)**, cover and leave to proof for 2–6 hours in a warm place (see page 25). **(H)**

7 After 2–6 hours, cracks will appear on the surface of the loaf and it should have increased in volume. **(I)**

8 At this point, preheat the oven to 250°C (500°F) Gas 9. Place a deep roasting tray at the bottom of the oven.

9 Place the loaf pan in the preheated oven. Pour a cup of water into the hot roasting tray and lower the temperature to 230°C (450°F) Gas 8.

10 Bake for 35–40 minutes until cooked through.

11 Tap the loaf on the bottom – it should sound hollow. If you are not sure, return it to the oven for a further 10 minutes.

12 Turn the loaf out of the loaf pan and allow to cool on a wire rack.

Teff and apricot sourdough

Teff is an ancient grain that is becoming ever more popular. In Ethiopia, it is a staple foodstuff used to make the flatbread injera. Unlike some other gluten-free flours, teff tastes great on its own so doesn't need to be mixed with other flours. This moist, flavoursome loaf will surprise you.

A

TIME PLANNER

Making the dough **10 minutes**

Letting the dough rise **8 hours**

Knocking back and shaping the dough **10 minutes**

Final proofing **2–6 hours**

Baking **35–40 minutes**

Cooling **30 minutes**

INGREDIENTS

250 g/2 scant cups teff flour

5 g/1 teaspoon salt

100 g/⅔ cup dried apricots, chopped into small pieces

12 g/½ oz. gluten-free sourdough starter (see pages 16–17). I've used teff.

320 g/320 ml/1⅓ cups warm water (30–37°C/86–99°F)

teff grains, for sprinkling

EQUIPMENT

1 x 500-g/1-lb. loaf pan, greased with vegetable or sunflower oil

Makes 1 x 500-g/1-lb. loaf

1 In a small mixing bowl, add the flour, salt and dried chopped apricots, and mix together thoroughly. This is the dry mixture.

2 Add the sourdough starter to a large mixing bowl with the warm water and dissolve or break it up with your hands.

3 Add the dry mixture, and mix it together until it forms a thick batter consistency. If it is too stiff, add more water and remember to record how much more water you used for next time.

4 Cover the dough and leave it to rise overnight in a cool place (not in the fridge, though).

5 The next day, deflate the dough by stirring it with a wooden spoon

6 Transfer the dough into the greased loaf pan and sprinkle some teff grains on top.

7 Cover with a shower cap or a large mixing bowl and allow the dough to proof for 2–6 hours. **(A)**

8 After 2–6 hours, cracks will have appeared on the surface of the loaf and it should have increased in volume. At this point, preheat the oven to 250°C (500°F) Gas 9. Place a deep roasting tray at the bottom of the oven.

9 Place the loaf pan in the preheated oven. Pour a cup of water into the hot roasting tray and lower the temperature to 230°C (450°F) Gas 8.

10 Bake for 35–40 minutes until cooked through.

11 Tap the loaf on the bottom. If you hear a hollow sound, it is ready. If you are not sure, return it to the oven for a further 10 minutes.

12 Turn the loaf out of the loaf pan and allow it to cool on a wire rack.

TIME PLANNER

Soaking the quinoa **8 hours**

Making the dough **10 minutes**

Letting the dough rise **8–12 hours**

Knocking back and shaping the dough **10 minutes**

Final proofing **2–6 hours**

Resting in the fridge **30 minutes**

Baking **25–35 minutes**

Cooling **30 minutes**

INGREDIENTS

100 g/1 cup plus 1 tablespoon red quinoa

160 g/1¼ cups quinoa flour, plus extra for dusting

8 g/¼ oz. psyllium husk

5 g/1 teaspoon salt

14 g/½ oz. quinoa sourdough starter (see pages 16–17)

150 g/150 ml/⅔ cup warm water (30–37°C/86–99°F)

EQUIPMENT

1 x 500-g/1-lb. long proofing/dough-rising basket

1 small peel, floured with buckwheat flour

Makes 1 x 500-g/1-lb. loaf

Red quinoa sourdough

This recipe was inspired by an online course taught by Chris Stafferton, a master of gluten-free baking. He introduced me to psyllium husk, a natural gelling agent compared with common alternatives like xanthan gum. The red quinoa grains give the inside a lovely speckled effect.

1 In a large mixing bowl, soak the quinoa grains in double their volume of cold water for 8 hours or overnight.

2 The next day, add the quinoa flour, psyllium husk and salt to a small mixing bowl, mix them together thoroughly and set aside. This is the dry mixture.

3 In a large mixing bowl, add the quinoa sourdough starter and the warm water. Break up the starter with your hands.

4 Drain the soaked quinoa, which will have begun to sprout, and rinse with cold water so that it does not taste bitter when baked.

5 Add the soaked quinoa to the sourdough mixture **(A)**. Add the dry mixture and mix everything together until it forms a soft mixture. **(B)**

6 Cover the dough and leave it to rise overnight in a cool place (not in the fridge, though). **(C)**

7 Remove the dough from the bowl, using a light sprinkling of quinoa flour so it does not stick. Shape into a ball **(D)** (see pages 24–25) and leave it to rest before rolling it into a long shape (see pages 28–29). Note that the consistency of the dough will be more putty-like than a loaf containing gluten.

8 Sprinkle some quinoa flour to coat the inside of the proofing/dough-rising basket. **(E)**

9 Place the dough seam-up into the basket. **(F)**

10 Leave to proof for 2–6 hours in a warm place (see page 25). Cover only if the warm place is draughty.

11 After 2–6 hours, cracks will appear on the surface of the loaf and it should have increased in volume.

12 When the loaf is ready for baking, place it in the fridge for 30 minutes to stabilize it.

13 Preheat the oven to 250°C (500°F) Gas 9. Place a deep roasting tray at the bottom of the oven and a baking sheet on the middle shelf.

14 Turn the dough out onto a peel floured with quinoa flour.

15 Slash the loaf with a sharp knife or a lamé to create a pattern of your choice.

16 Slide the loaf onto the preheated baking sheet in the oven. Pour a cup of water into the hot roasting tray.

17 Bake for 35–40 minutes until cooked through. Check the loaf after 15 minutes and if it is getting too dark, lower the temperature to 230°C (450°F) Gas 8.

18 Tap the loaf on the bottom. If you hear a hollow sound, it is ready. If you are not sure, return it to the oven for a further 10 minutes.

19 Remove the loaf from the baking sheet and allow it to cool on a wire rack.

Note: You can bake a slightly different version of this loaf by increasing the amount of quinoa sourdough starter to 90 g/ 3 oz. rather than 14 g/½ oz. In this version, the dough only needs to rise (the first time) for 1 hour and should be covered. Then follow steps 7–19.

A

B

Chickpea and potato focaccia

This is a great gluten-free variant of a focaccia. While it won't have the same open texture as a traditional focaccia, it does have a lovely nutty flavour and a moreishly light consistency.

1 Add the potato flour, chickpea/gram flour, rosemary and salt to a small mixing bowl, mix them together thoroughly with a wooden spoon and set aside. This is the dry mixture.

2 In a large mixing bowl, add the gluten-free sourdough starter and ¾ of the warm water. Mix it together until the sourdough starter dissolves. Mix in the grated potato.

3 Add the dry mixture to the dissolved sourdough, mixing it together until it forms a batter mixture. If the dough feels a little on the stiff side, add the rest of the remaining water.

4 Cover and leave the dough to rise for 1 hour in a warm place (see page 25).

5 Pour the mixture onto the lined baking sheet. Decorate with sprigs of rosemary and a light sprinkling of coarse salt.

6 Leave to proof for 1–3 hours in a warm place again. Cover if the room is draughty.

7 After 1–3 hours, you will notice cracks appearing on the surface of the loaf and it should have increased in volume.

8 At this point, preheat the oven to 250°C (500°F) Gas 9. Place a deep roasting tray at the bottom of the oven.

9 Drizzle with loaf with olive oil. Place the baking sheet in the preheated oven and pour a cup of water into the hot roasting tray.

10 Bake for 15–20 minutes until cooked through. Check the loaf after 15 minutes and if it is getting too dark, lower the temperature to 230°C (450°F) Gas 8.

11 Tap the bottom of the loaf – it should sound hollow. If you are not sure, return it to the oven for a further 10 minutes.

12 Remove the loaf from the baking sheet and allow it cool on a wire rack.

TIME PLANNER

Making the dough **10 minutes**

Letting the dough rise **1 hour**

Knocking back, shaping and decorating the dough **10 minutes**

Final proofing **1–3 hours**

Baking **15–20 minutes**

Cooling **30 minutes**

INGREDIENTS

130 g/1 scant cup potato flour/potato starch

130 g/1 cup chickpea/gram flour

3 g/⅛ teaspoon chopped fresh rosemary, plus extra rosemary sprigs for topping

6 g/1 teaspoon salt

100 g/3½ oz. gluten-free sourdough starter (see pages 16–17)

130 g/130 ml/scant ½ cup warm water (30–37°C/86–99°F)

100 g/¾ cup finely grated raw potato

coarse salt, for topping

olive oil, for topping

EQUIPMENT

1 x rectangular baking sheet (27 x 18 x 3 cm/11 x 7 x 1 inches), lined with baking parchment

Makes 1 x 800-g/1¾-lbs. loaf

TIME PLANNER

Making the mixture and leaving to rest **45 minutes**

Frying the pancakes **15 minutes**

Cooling **5 minutes**

INGREDIENTS

50 g/3 tablespoons chickpea/ gram flour

50 g/3 tablespoons potato flour/ potato starch or tapioca flour

50 g/3 tablespoons brown rice flour

8 g/1½ teaspoons salt

200 g/1½ cups finely grated raw potato

100 g/¾ cup finely sliced red onion

16 g/½ oz. crushed or very finely grated garlic

5 g/1 teaspoon cumin seeds

150 g/5½ oz. gluten-free sourdough starter (see pages 16–17)

100 g/100 ml/7 tablespoons warm water (30–37°C/86–99°F)

zest of 1 lemon

6 g/1 teaspoon baking powder

vegetable or sunflower oil, for frying

EQUIPMENT

1 griddle pan or heavy-based frying pan/skillet

Makes 5 large or 10 small pancakes

Potato and chickpea sourdough pancakes

This recipe has been a hit whenever I've tried it. The garlic, onion and potato combination make it a lovely savoury treat, and it's not too heavy. The lemon gives it a nice zing which goes well with the earthy cumin. It's great with a dollop of cream cheese and chopped fresh chives.

1 In a small mixing bowl, mix the flours with the salt. This is the dry mixture.

2 In another small mixing bowl, mix the grated raw potato, onion, garlic and the cumin seeds.

3 In a large mixing bowl, dissolve or break up the sourdough starter in the warm water.

4 Add the dry mixture and potato mixture to the dissolved sourdough starter and mix until thoroughly combined. Leave the mixture for 30 minutes to develop flavour.

5 Add the baking powder and the lemon zest. Leave the mixture to rest for 10 minutes before frying.

6 To fry the pancakes, lightly grease a griddle pan or frying pan/skillet and place over a medium heat until a drop of batter sizzles on contact with the pan/skillet.

7 Drop a quantity of batter into the pan and cook until the top of the pancake is no longer wet **(A)**. Turn the pancake over with a thin spatula or palette knife and cook the other side until it is lightly browned. **(B)**

8 Keep the pancakes warm by stacking them on a serving plate. Eat them immediately!

SOURDOUGH TREATS

Sourdough bagels and pretzels

This recipe for bagels and pretzels – the ultimate filling, versatile snacks – involves making the same dough and dividing it into six pieces. The difference comes afterwards. The instructions for shaping, boiling and baking bagels are on page 114, with the pretzel instructions on page 116.

The instructions for shaping, boiling and baking bagels are on page 114, with the pretzel instructions on page 116.

TIME PLANNER

Making the dough **50 minutes**

Letting the dough rise **8–12 hours**

Knocking back and shaping the dough **10–20 minutes**

Boiling the bagels or dipping the pretzels **10 minutes**

Final proofing **15 minutes**

Baking **15 minutes**

Cooling **15 minutes**

INGREDIENTS

500 g/3½ cups white strong/bread flour, plus extra for dusting

10 g/2 teaspoons salt

20 g/4 teaspoons caster/superfine sugar

25 g/2 tablespoons butter (salted or unsalted)

25 g/1 oz. sourdough starter (see pages 16–17)

200 g/200 ml/¾ cup warm water (30–37°C/86–99°F)

1 egg, beaten

EQUIPMENT

1 baking sheet lined with baking parchment

Makes 6 bagels or pretzels

1 In a small mixing bowl, mix the flour, salt, sugar and butter together thoroughly and set aside. This is the dry mixture.

2 Add the sourdough starter to a large mixing bowl. Add ¾ of the warm water and dissolve or break up the sourdough with your hands.

3 Add the beaten egg and dry mixture to the dissolved sourdough and stir the mixture slowly with your hands until it comes together and there are no dry bits at the bottom of the bowl.

4 At this point the dough should come together and be slightly sticky but stiff. If the dough doesn't come together and seems a bit dry, add a little or all of the remaining water.

5 Cover the mixture with the small mixing bowl. Leave to stand for 10 minutes.

6 Knead the mixture 10 times (see page 22).

7 Turn the ball of dough over in the bowl and make a finger mark in the dough (to indicate the first knead).

8 Cover with the small mixing bowl that had the flour in it and leave the dough to rest for 10 minutes.

9 Repeat steps 6–8 another 3 times, making sure the mixture is covered between kneads and remembering to mark the dough to indicate the number of kneads done. If the dough starts to resist and starts to tear, apply less pressure as you knead. If the dough becomes difficult to knead after kneading it 8 times, stop.

10 Cover the dough and leave it to rise overnight in a cool place (not in the fridge, though).

11 The next day, gently punch down to de-gas the dough.

12 Remove from the bowl, using a light sprinkling of flour so the dough does not stick. Divide the mixture into 6 equal portions and roll into balls, cover and leave to rest for 10 minutes.

A

SHAPING, BOILING AND BAKING THE BAGELS

1 kg/1 litre/4 cups water and 5 g/1 teaspoon salt

egg wash made from 1 lightly beaten egg and a pinch of salt

poppy seeds or sesame seeds, for topping

1 Place the water and salt in a large saucepan and boil.

2 Shape the balls by pressing a hole through the middle and widening it with your fingers **(A)**. Place on the prepared baking sheet and allow to rest for 15 minutes **(B)**.

3 Place the bagels into the boiling water **(C)**. When the bagels rise up (after roughly 5 minutes), turn them over and boil for a further 5 minutes, turning them over twice in that time.

4 Place the bagels back on the baking sheet and allow to cool slightly.

5 Use a pastry brush to apply egg wash to the bagels **(D)**. To make seeded bagels, dip the bagels in poppy or sesame seeds and place back on the baking sheet. **(E)**

6 Preheat the oven to 250°C (500°F) Gas 9 and place a deep roasting tray at the bottom of the oven.

7 Place the baking sheet in the preheated oven. Pour a cup of water into the hot roasting tray and lower the temperature to 230°C (450°F) Gas 8.

8 Bake for 15 minutes until golden brown and allow to cool.

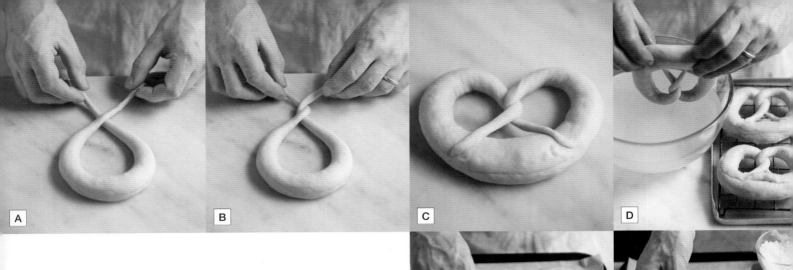

SHAPING AND BAKING THE PRETZELS

coarse salt, for topping

Dipping mixture

1 kg/1 litre/4 cups water

40 g/8 teaspoons salt

100 g/¾ cup bicarbonate of/baking soda

1 Add the dipping mixture ingredients to a large saucepan and bring to the boil. Once the mixture boils, remove from the heat and allow to cool.

2 Shape each dough portion into a small sausage and allow to rest for about 10 minutes.

3 Roll each piece until it is about 30 cm/12 inches long with the middle part thicker, tapering into a point at both ends.

4 Once you have rolled all the pieces, shape them into pretzels. Start by making an 'n' shape, then cross the pointy ends and twist leaving about 2 cm/¾ inch space between the twist and the pointed end. **(A) (B)**

5 Pick up the twisted part and press it back into the thicker part of the dough (at roughly ten and two o'clock positions) **(C)**, leaving a gap of about 3 cm/1 inch. Place it on the prepared baking sheet.

6 Repeat steps 4–5 to shape the remaining pretzels.

7 Carefully pick up each pretzel, holding it by the places

where you have stuck the points together, and dip it into the dipping mixture. The pretzels will stretch a little as you do this. **(D)**

8 Repeat the dipping process another 2 times, giving the dipping mixture time to dry before you dip the pretzels again.

9 After the last dip, sprinkle some coarse salt on the top and allow the pretzels to proof for 15 minutes then place them in the fridge to form a skin for 15–20 minutes.

10 Preheat the oven to 250°C (500°F) Gas 9 and place a deep roasting tray on the bottom of the oven.

11 Slash the pretzel tops with a sharp serrated knife or a lamé **(E)** and sprinkle the cut area with some more coarse salt **(F)**.

12 Place the baking sheet in the oven. Pour a cup of water into the hot roasting tray.

13 Bake for 15 minutes until golden brown. Check the pretzels after 10 minutes. If they are getting too dark, lower the temperature to 230°C (450°F) Gas 8. Cool on a wire rack.

Sourdough croissants

People ask me why it's worth making a sourdough croissant when you can make a perfectly good yeasted one. The reason is down to the flavour, which reaches another level and has converted many a sceptic. In my experience, they seem to disappear quicker than yeasted ones.

TIME PLANNER

Making the pre-ferment **8–9 hours**

Making the dough **50 minutes**

Letting the dough rise **2 hours**

Resting in the fridge **8 hours**

Knocking back and laminating the dough **2 hours**

Rolling out and cutting **15 minutes**

Final proofing **2–3 hours**

Baking **15–25 minutes**

Cooling **10 minutes**

INGREDIENTS

180 g/1¼ cups white strong/bread flour, plus extra for sprinkling

5 g/1 teaspoon salt

20 g/4 teaspoons caster/superfine sugar

20 g/4 teaspoons butter, chopped into small pieces, plus 150 g/1¼ sticks butter, refrigerated

70 g/70 ml/5 tablespoons warm milk (30–37°C/ 86–99°F)

egg wash made from 1 lightly beaten egg and a pinch of salt

For the pre-ferment

70 g/½ cup white strong/bread flour

10 g/2 teaspoons caster/superfine sugar

75 g/2½ oz. sourdough starter (see pages 16–17)

70 g/70 ml/5 tablespoons warm water (30–37°C/86–99°F)

EQUIPMENT

1 baking sheet lined with baking parchment

Makes 8

1 To make the pre-ferment, add the flour and sugar to a small mixing bowl, mix and set aside. In a large mixing bowl, dissolve or break up the sourdough starter in the warm water. Add the flour and sugar mixture and mix together to make a paste consistency. Scrape around the edges of the bowl and cover with the small mixing bowl. Leave to ferment in a cool place (not in the fridge, though) for 8–9 hours.

2 While the pre-ferment rises, add the flour, salt, sugar and chopped butter to another small mixing bowl and set aside. This is the dry mixture.

3 After 8–9 hours, the pre-ferment should be bubbling. If not, leave to ferment for another hour until it is bubbling.

4 Uncover the bubbling pre-ferment and add the warm milk and the dry mixture. Mix everything with your hands until it comes together. The dough should be a little stiff. Cover with the small mixing bowl and leave to stand for 10 minutes.

5 Knead the mixture 10 times (see page 22).

6 Turn the ball of dough over in the bowl and make a finger mark in the dough (to indicate the first knead).

7 Cover with the small mixing bowl and leave the dough to rest for 10 minutes.

8 Repeat steps 5–7 another 3 times, making sure the mixture is covered between kneads and remembering to mark the dough to indicate the amount of kneads done. If the dough starts to resist and starts to tear, apply less pressure as you knead. If the dough becomes difficult to knead after kneading it 8 times, stop.

9 You are looking for a smooth, stiff elastic dough. If you think the dough is not kneaded enough, repeat steps 5–7 another time.

10 Cover and leave the dough to rise for 2 hours in a warm place (see page 25).

11 Place the dough in the fridge overnight and re-cover. Shape the remaining butter into a flat rectangle about 12 cm/5 inches long by 7 cm/3 inches wide and 2 cm/ ¾ inch thick and place in the fridge.

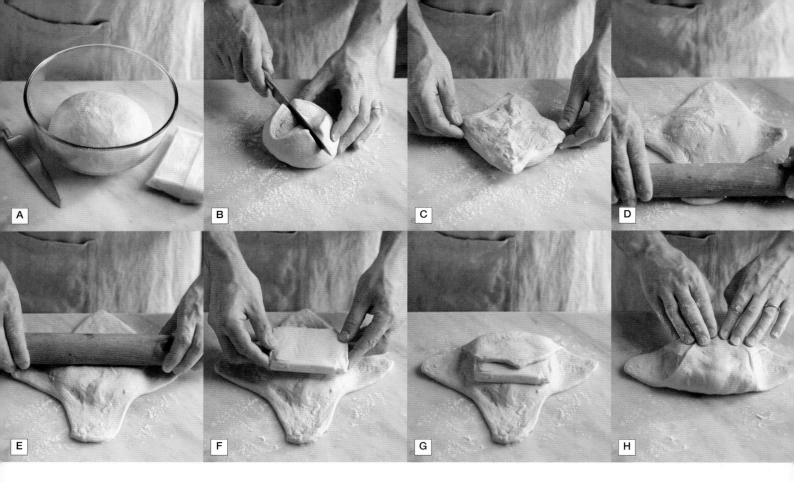

12 The next day, remove the dough from the fridge, using a light sprinkling of flour so the dough does not stick. Also remove the butter from the fridge. **(A)**

13 Shape the dough into a ball. First, flatten the dough slightly with your palm.

14 Take a corner of the dough and fold it right over to the opposite side then turn the dough 90° clockwise.

15 Repeat the previous step 4–5 more times until the dough is a roundish shape.

16 Turn the dough over and keeping tucking in the underneath of the dough with your fingers as you rotate the dough clockwise until you've formed a rounded ball.

17 Make a cross-cut on the surface, cutting about half-way into the dough. **(B)**

18 The butter should now be at room temperature and have softened a little (i.e. not so soft that you can press you finger straight through, but soft enough so that when you press your finger in it, it makes a dent in the butter.)

19 Pull the corners of the cut dough out to make a square with 4 triangular ears. **(C)**

20 Use a rolling pin to roll the dough to about the same thickness as the butter, but make it slightly thinner on the 4 triangular ears. **(D) (E)**

21 Place the butter in the middle of the square of dough. If it does not fit, roll the dough a bit bigger. **(F)**

22 Fold the corners of the dough to the centre, so that it is like a closed envelope with the butter in the middle. **(G) (H) (I) (J)**

23 Gently flatten the dough with a rolling pin, making sure the butter is dispersed everywhere in the envelope of dough and butter. **(K)**

24 Use the rolling pin to roll the dough into a long rectangular shape about 1 cm/½ inch thick. **(L) (M)**

25 Fold the bottom half of the dough to the centre, then fold the other half on top. **(N)**

26 You should have 3 rectangular pieces of dough piled on top of each other; this is your first turn. Press your finger into the centre of the dough to mark it. **(O)**

27 Cover the dough with a sheet of parchment paper and place it in the fridge for 20–30 minutes.

28 Remove from the fridge and repeat (steps 24–27) another 3 times so you will have given the dough 4 turns. **(P)**

29 Allow to rest for a further 20–30 minutes in the fridge. This will help make the pastry easier to roll out, stop the butter from getting too soft and prevent the dough from rising too much. If this does happen, place it in the freezer for 10 minutes to make it easier to work with.

30 Roll the pastry out to about 45 cm/17½ inches long by 21 cm/8½ inches wide and about 3 mm/⅛ inch thick.

31 Follow the instructions on pages 122–123 to shape and bake the croissants.

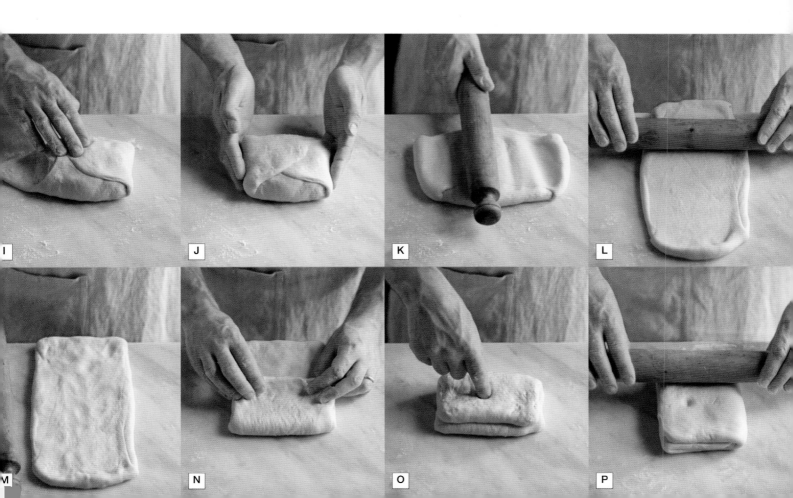

I   J   K   L

M   N   O   P

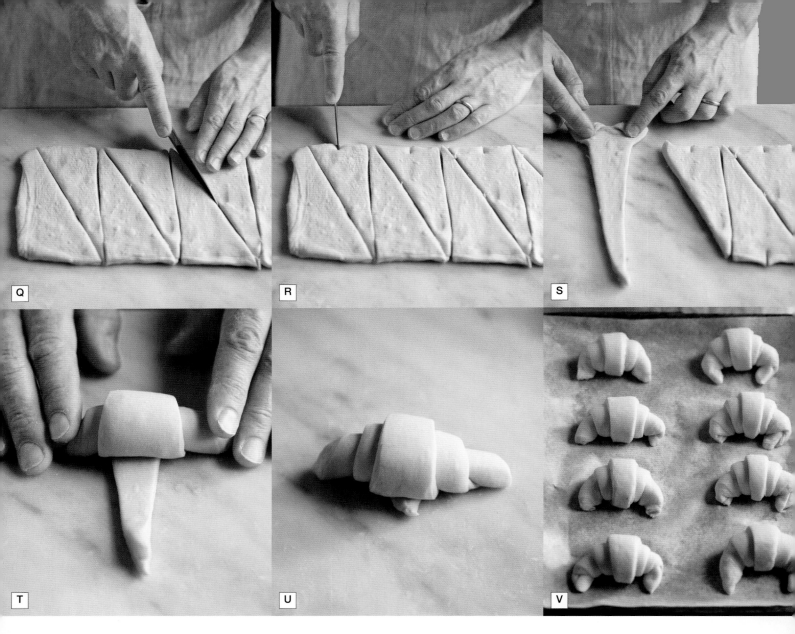

32 Divide the pastry into 4 equal portions, then cut each portion into 2 triangles, so you have 8 triangles in total **(Q)**.

33 Make a small cut about ½ cm/¼ inch deep in the middle of the bottom of each triangle **(R)**. Place a triangle in front of you with the point at the top. Stretch the bottom part of the triangle so the little cut becomes an upside-down 'v' and the two corners of the triangle form rounded edges. **(S)**

34 Roll each croissant up from the bottom end up, placing pressure on the sides until it is fully rolled up. **(T) (U)**

35 Place the croissants on the prepared baking sheet, at least 2 cm/¾ inch away from each other, and use a pastry brush to paint them with the egg wash. **(V) (X)**

36 Allow the croissants to rise in a warm place (see page 25) until you see the folds in the pastry separating and the croissants have increased in volume. This should take 2–3 hours, but check how they are doing every 30–40 minutes.

37 Preheat the oven to 250°C (500°F) Gas 9 and place a deep roasting tray at the bottom of the oven.

38 Lightly paint the croissants with the egg wash for the second time.

39 Place the baking sheet in the oven and pour a cup of water into the hot roasting tray to form steam. Lower the temperature to 200°C (400°F) Gas 6.

40 Bake for 15–25 minutes until golden brown. Allow to cool.

Fruit danishes and tartlets

1 Follow steps 1–29 on pages 119–121.

2 Make an almond filling by mixing 80 g/¾ cup ground almonds, 40 g/2½ tablespoons sugar and 40 g/40 ml/2½ tablespoons water until it forms a paste. Cover and set aside.

3 Roll the pastry out to 40 cm/16½ inches long by 20 cm/ 8 inches wide and about 3 mm/⅛ inch thick. Divide the dough into eight 10 x 10-cm/4 x 4-inch pieces.

4 **To make 4 pinwheel danishes**, take a square of pastry and make four 2 cm/¾ inch cuts at each corner **(A)**. Fold one of the 8 points into the centre, rotate to the right and fold not the next point but the one after that into the centre. Repeat until you have folded 4 points into the middle. **(B)**

5 Place the danishes at least 2 cm/¾ inch apart on the prepared baking sheet. Fill a piping bag with the almond filling and pipe it into the middle of each danish **(C)**. Decorate with slices of fresh apple. **(D)**

6 **To make 4 tartlets**, take one square of pastry **(E)** and fold it in half, point to point. Make a ½-cm/¼-in. long cut, (don't get too close to the point of the triangle) **(F)** through both layers, and another on the other side of the triangle. Unfold the triangle **(G)**. Fold the left corner to the opposite corner then repeat the other side **(H) (I)**. Fill a piping bag with the almond filling and pipe into the middle of each tartlet. **(J)**

7 Leave to rise for 2–3 hours in a warm place until the folds in the pastry separate and the danishes increase in volume.

8 Preheat the oven to 250°C (500°F) Gas 9 and place a roasting tray at the bottom of the oven. Place the baking sheet in the preheated oven and pour a cup of water into the hot roasting tray. Lower the oven temperature to 200°C (400°F) Gas 6.

9 Bake for 15–25 minutes until golden brown. Allow to cool. Glaze with hot apricot jam and decorate with fresh fruit.

Sourdough brioche

The egg and butter mixture gives the inside of this classic French treat its rich and luxurious texture and flavour. This sourdough version makes for a perfect treat at any time of day. I've made it in a large fluted cupcake pan, which looks really eye-catching and appetizing when baked.

TIME PLANNER

Making the pre-ferment **4 hours**

Making the dough **50 minutes**

Letting the dough rise **4 hours**

Knocking back and shaping the dough **10 minutes**

Final proofing **4–6 hours**

Baking **35–50 minutes**

Cooling **30 minutes**

INGREDIENTS

400 g/scant 3 cups white strong/bread flour, plus extra for dusting

20 g/4 teaspoons caster/granulated sugar

8 g/1½ teaspoons salt

4 eggs, lightly beaten

160 g/1⅓ sticks butter (salted or unsalted), softened

egg wash made from 1 lightly beaten egg and a pinch of salt

pearl or nibbed sugar, for decoration

For the pre-ferment

120 g/1 scant cup white strong/bread flour

12 g/2½ teaspoons caster/superfine sugar

40 g/1½ oz. sourdough starter (see pages 16–17)

120 g/120 ml/½ cup warm milk (30–37°C/86–99°F)

EQUIPMENT

1 x 400-g/14-oz. round loaf pan or 22-cm/9-inch fluted cupcake pan, buttered

Makes 1 large brioche

1 To make the pre-ferment, first add the flour and sugar to a small mixing bowl and set aside. In a large mixing bowl, dissolve or break up the sourdough starter in the warm milk, add the flour mixture and mix together to make a paste consistency. Cover with an upturned small mixing bowl and leave to ferment in a warm place (see page 25) for about 4 hours.

2 In another small mixing bowl, mix the remaining flour, sugar and salt together and set aside. This is the dry mixture.

3 After 4 hours, the pre-ferment should be bubbling. If not, leave to ferment for a further hour until it is bubbling.

4 Uncover the pre-ferment and add the lightly beaten eggs (A). Add the dry mixture (B) and mix until it comes together (C) (D). At this point the dough will be slightly sticky.

5 Place the softened butter on top of the sticky dough. Cover the mixture with the small mixing bowl and leave to stand for 10 minutes. (E)

6 Knead the mixture 10 times (see page 22). Start by squashing the butter into the dough with your knuckles and fingers to incorporate it into the dough. The mixture will get more sticky as you work the butter into the dough. (F) (G)

7 Turn the ball of dough over in the bowl and make a finger mark in the dough (to indicate the first knead).

8 Cover with the small mixing bowl and leave the dough to rest for 10 minutes.

9 Repeat steps 6–8 another 3 times, making sure the mixture is covered between kneads and remembering to mark the dough to indicate the number of kneads done. You should have incorporated all the butter into the dough by now. (H)

10 Cover the dough with a shower cap or with the mixing bowl that had the flour in it and leave it to rise for 4 hours in a warm place again.

11 After 4 hours, you will notice that the dough has risen (I). Remove the dough from the bowl and place it on a work surface that has been dusted with a light sprinkling of flour. Shape the dough into the desired shape and place into a buttered loaf pan. Alternatively, shape the dough into a ball (see pages 24–25) and place it in a large fluted cupcake pan. (J)

12 Cover again and let the brioche rise in a warm place again for 4–6 hours.

13 After 4–6 hours the brioche should have nearly doubled in volume. If you feel it has not risen enough, leave to rise for a further 1–2 hours.

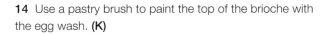

14 Use a pastry brush to paint the top of the brioche with the egg wash. **(K)**

15 Sprinkle a handful of pearl or nibbed sugar on the top for decoration. **(L)**

16 Preheat the oven to 250°C (500°F) Gas 9 and place a deep roasting tray at the bottom of the oven.

17 Place the brioche in the preheated oven. Pour a cup of water into the hot roasting tray, and lower the oven temperature to 200°C (400°F) Gas 6.

18 Bake for 35–50 minutes until golden brown.

19 Carefully remove the brioche from the pan and tap on the bottom. If you hear a hollow sound, it is ready. If you are not sure, return it to the oven for a further 10 minutes.

20 If it is ready, allow it to cool on a wire rack. **(M)**

SPECIALITY SOURDOUGHS

A B C D

Sourdough baguette

This classic sourdough baguette includes both white strong/bread flour and plain/all-purpose flour to imitate the medium to strong French flour used to make traditional baguettes. I've also included a variant method for an 'epi' baguette – a beautiful baguette shaped like an ear of wheat.

TIME PLANNER

Making the pre-ferment **8 hours**

Making the dough **50 minutes**

Letting the dough rise **1 hour**

Pre-shaping the dough **15 minutes**

Rolling the dough **10 minutes**

Final proofing **30–60 minutes**

Resting in the fridge **30 minutes**

Baking **15–25 minutes**

Cooling **30 minutes**

INGREDIENTS

300 g/2¼ cups plain/all-purpose flour, plus extra for dusting

9 g/2 teaspoons salt

150 g/150 ml/⅔ cup warm water

For the pre-ferment

10 g/⅓ oz. sourdough starter (see pages 16–17)

125 g/125 ml/½ cup warm water

125 g/1 scant cup white strong/bread flour

EQUIPMENT

proofing linen or tea/dish towel

Makes 3 baguettes

1 To make the pre-ferment, in a large mixing bowl, dissolve or break up the sourdough starter in the warm water. Add the flour and mix together to form a paste consistency. Cover with a small mixing bowl and leave to ferment at room temperature for 8 hours or overnight.

2 Put the flour and the salt in a small mixing bowl and set aside. This is the dry mixture.

3 The next day (or after 8 hours), uncover the pre-ferment, which should be bubbling and have a pleasant smell. If it is not bubbling, place in a warm place until it starts to bubble.

4 When the pre-ferment is bubbling, add the warm water, loosen the mixture from the bowl and add the dry mixture. Mix until it all comes together and there are no dry bits at the bottom of the bowl. At this point the dough should be slightly sticky.

5 Cover the mixture with the small mixing bowl and leave to stand for 10 minutes.

6 Knead the mixture 10 times (page 22).

7 Turn the ball of dough over in the bowl and make a finger mark in the dough (to indicate the first knead).

8 Cover with the small mixing bowl and leave the dough to rest for 10 minutes.

9 Repeat steps 6–8 another 3 times, making sure the mixture is covered between kneads and remembering to mark the dough to indicate the number of kneads done. If the dough starts to resist and starts to tear, apply less pressure as you knead. If the dough becomes difficult to knead after kneading it 8 times, stop.

10 Cover the dough and leave it to rise for 1 hour. **(A)**

11 After 1 hour, lightly sprinkle some white flour on a work surface and place the dough onto it.

12 Use a metal dough scraper to cut the dough into 3 pieces. **(B)**

13 Gently flatten each piece of dough into an oval. Pull both ends of the oval out, then fold them over into the middle. You will now have a roughly rectangular shape. **(C) (D)**

14 Pull and fold the top of the rectangle one-third of the way towards the middle, pressing it into the dough. Swivel it 180° and repeat. Repeat until you have a neat, long loaf shape **(E) (F)**. Repeat with the remaining portions of dough.

15 Cover the loaves (seam-side down) and let rest for 15 minutes. **(G: the pre-shape)**

16 Turn one loaf over and flatten slightly. Fold the top right of the rectangle one-third of the way towards the middle, pressing it into the dough. Repeat with the top left and repeat until rolled up **(H) (I)**. Repeat with the remaining portions of dough.

17 Roll the dough between your hands until you get a baguette about the length of your baking sheet or the desired length. Repeat with the remaining portions of dough. **(J)**

18 Dust the proofing linen or clean tea/dish towel with flour and lay it on the baking sheet. Arrange the baguettes on the cloth, seam-side up, pulling a bit of excess cloth between each baguette to separate them. **(K)**

19 Cover with a cloth and allow to proof for 30–60 minutes or until they have nearly doubled in volume.

20 Place the baguettes in the fridge for 30 minutes.

21 Preheat the oven to 250°C (500°F) Gas 9 and place a deep roasting tray at the bottom of the oven and a baking sheet on the middle shelf.

22 Remove the baguettes from the fridge and turn the baguettes over, seam-side down, onto a floured peel. Dust the baguettes with flour.

23 Slash the baguettes with a sharp serrated knife or a lamé to create a pattern of your choice. **(L)**

24 Slide the baguettes onto the preheated baking sheet in the oven and pour a cup of water into the hot roasting tray.

25 Bake for 15–25 minutes until golden brown. To check if baked through, tip one loaf upside down and tap the bottom – it should sound hollow. Set on a wire rack to cool.

Variation: If you are making 'Epi' baguettes, follow steps 1–19 and place the dough on a work surface. Cut the dough from one end with a sharp pair of scissors at a 30–45° angle between the peel and the scissors until you are about 5 mm/ ¼ inch from the work surface. Be careful not to cut all the way through the dough. Lay the piece you've cut over to one side. Continue to cut and turn in this way **(M)** until you've reached the other end. You should have 6–8 segments. Follow steps 21–25. **(N: the finished epi and regular baguettes)**

E

F

G

H

I

J

K

L

Sourdough ciabatta

This well-known Italian bread is named after its appearance ('ciabatta' means 'slipper' in Italian). Making this classic bread is a little bit like alchemy. It starts off unappealing and messy and turns slowly into something wonderful!

TIME PLANNER

Making the dough **10 minutes**

Letting the dough rise **1 hour**

Folding and resting the dough **5 hours**

Shaping the dough **10 minutes**

Final proofing **10–15 minutes**

Baking **20–30 minutes**

Cooling **30 minutes**

INGREDIENTS

500 g/3½ cups white strong/bread flour or '00' Italian bread-making flour, plus extra for dusting

10 g/2 teaspoons salt

150 g/5½ oz. sourdough starter (see pages 16–17)

400 g/400 ml/1⅔ cups warm water (30–37°C/86–99°F)

30 g/30 ml/6 teaspoons olive oil, for folding

Makes 3 ciabatta loaves

1 In a small mixing bowl, mix the flour and salt together and set aside. This is the dry mixture.

2 In a large mixing bowl, dissolve or break up the sourdough starter in the warm water. This is the wet mixture.

3 Add the dry mixture to the wet mixture. Mix together thoroughly until a fairly sticky dough forms.

4 Pour half of the olive oil into another large mixing bowl, coating the bottom of the bowl.

5 Transfer the sticky dough into the large mixing bowl containing the oil **(A)**, cover **(B)** and allow to rest for 1 hour in a warm place. The olive oil is used to add flavour and to ensure that the dough does not stick to the bowl.

6 After 1 hour, lightly fold the dough twice. Do this by stretching the dough and folding one side to the centre, then rotate the bowl 180° and fold one side to the centre again. **(C)**

7 Rotate the bowl 90° and lightly fold the dough again twice (so you will have done 4 folds in total), then turn the dough over. If you find the dough sticks to the bowl, add a little of the remaining olive oil.

8 Repeat steps 6–7 another 3 times, remembering to cover and rest the dough for 1 hour in between folds, adding extra olive oil if the dough sticks to the bowl. Leave the dough in a warm place to rise for 1 hour.

9 When the dough has risen and is nice and bubbly **(D)**, tip onto a well-floured work surface **(E)**, making sure not to damage the air bubbles. Coat the top with flour as well.

10 Fold the dough into a rectangular shape, then flip it over and tuck in the underneath. It should be a fairly fat rectangle **(F) (G)**, which will help you cut it into 3 equal pieces.

11 Preheat the oven to 250°C (500°F) Gas 9 and place a heavy baking sheet on the middle shelf.

12 Cut the dough into three slipper-shaped rectangular loaves using a metal dough scraper **(H)**. Roll the loaves in flour.

13 Let the loaves rest for 10–15 minutes.

14 Remove the hot baking sheet from the oven and place it on a cooling rack.

15 Transfer the ciabatta loaves to the hot baking sheet and place back in the oven.

16 Bake for 20–30 minutes.

17 Check that the loaves are done by tipping upside down and tapping on the bottom. If you hear a hollow sound, it's ready. If not, return to the oven briefly.

18 Allow the ciabatta loaves to cool on a wire rack.

Note: If you want to make a flavoured ciabatta, add olives, sundried tomato etc., to the dough at step 12, fold the top over and pinch the sides together. Make sure the ingredients are added to the part of the dough that has no flour on it.

Sourdough tsoureki

TIME PLANNER

Making the pre-ferment **4 hours**

Making the dough **50 minutes**

Letting the dough rise **4 hours**

Knocking back and shaping the dough **10 minutes**

Final proofing **4–6 hours**

Baking **25–35 minutes**

Cooling **30 minutes**

INGREDIENTS

100 g/1 stick minus 1 tablespoon unsalted butter

90 g/scant ½ cup caster/superfine sugar

10 g/2 teaspoons mahleb (mahlepi)

10 g/2 teaspoons ground cardamom

zest of 2 oranges

2 eggs

350 g/2½ cups white strong/bread flour, plus extra for dusting

4 g/1 teaspoon salt

egg wash, made from 1 beaten egg mixed with a pinch of salt

sesame seeds or sliced almonds, for topping (optional)

For the pre-ferment

70 g/½ cup white strong/bread flour

15 g/1 tablespoon caster/superfine sugar

100 g/3½ oz. sourdough starter (see pages 16–17)

70 g/70 ml/5 tablespoons warm milk (30–37°C/86–99°F)

EQUIPMENT

1 x baking sheet lined with parchment paper or a 800-g/1¾-lb. loaf pan, greased with vegetable or sunflower oil

Makes 1 x 800-g/1¾-lb. loaf

Tsoureki is a Greek speciality and is traditionally eaten at Easter. This pretty loaf may look daunting but it's easy once you've mastered the simple plaiting/braiding technique. My tsoureki is flavoured with cardamom, orange zest and mahleb (ground cherry pips, which are popular in Middle Eastern cooking).

1 To make the pre-ferment, first add the flour and sugar to a small mixing bowl and set aside. In a large mixing bowl, dissolve or break up the sourdough in the warm milk. Add the flour and sugar mixture and mix together to make a paste consistency. Scrape around the edges of the mixing bowl and cover with the upturned small mixing bowl. Leave to ferment in a warm place for 4 hours.

2 Mix the sugar, mahleb (mahlepi), cardamom and orange zest together in a small mixing bowl and set aside. This mixture is best put together just before you make the dough.

3 Melt the butter in a saucepan. Once the butter has melted, remove from the heat and add the sugar and mahleb mixture, mixing thoroughly. Allow the mixture to cool.

4 When the butter and sugar mixture is cool, whisk in the eggs and mix until combined thoroughly. Set aside.

5 After 4 hours, the pre-ferment should be bubbling. If not, leave to ferment for a further hour until it is bubbling.

6 In another small mixing bowl, mix the flour and salt together and set aside. This is the dry mixture.

7 Add the dry mixture to the pre-ferment, add the butter and egg mixture and mix until it all comes together.

8 At this point, the dough should come together and be slightly sticky and stiff. Cover the mixture with the upturned small mixing bowl.

9 Leave to stand for 10 minutes.

10 Knead the mixture 10 times (see page 22).

11 Turn the ball of dough over in the bowl and make a finger mark in the dough (to indicate the first knead),

12 Cover with the small mixing bowl and leave the dough to rest for 10 minutes.

13 Repeat steps 11–13 another 3 times, making sure the mixture is covered between kneads and remembering to mark the dough to indicate the number of kneads done. If the dough starts to resist and starts to tear, apply less pressure as you knead. If the dough becomes difficult to knead after kneading it 8 times, stop.

14 The dough should be smooth and elastic. If you think it is not kneaded enough repeat steps 11–13 another time.

15 Cover and leave the dough to rise for 4 hours in a warm place.

16 Using a light sprinkling of flour, divide the dough into 4 equal pieces.

17 Roll out each piece of dough into a sausage shape about 25 cm/10 inches long, tapered at the end.

18 Lay out the pieces on a work surface, side by side, in a 'v' shape and press the ends together at the base of the 'v' to seal.

19 Now refer to the step-by-step pictures on the opposite page to plait/braid the lengths of dough into a tsoureki shape. Make sure the ends of the tsoureki are neatly tucked in.

20 Place the loaf onto a baking sheet lined with baking parchment or into a greased loaf pan.

21 Cover and allow the loaf to rise for 4–6 hours in a cool place (not in the fridge, though).

22 After about 6 hours, the loaf should have risen slightly less than double in volume. If you feel it has not risen enough, leave for a further 1–2 hours until it is ready.

23 Brush the top with egg wash using a pastry brush. I left my tsoureki plain, but you could also sprinkle some sesame seeds or sliced almonds on top if you like.

24 Preheat the oven to 230°C (450°F) Gas 8 and place a deep roasting tray at the bottom of the oven.

25 Place the baking sheet or loaf pan in the preheated oven and pour a cup of water into the hot roasting tray to form steam. Lower the oven temperature to 180°C (360°F) Gas 4.

26 Bake for 25–35 minutes until golden brown. Check the loaf after 10–15 minutes as it can become dark very quickly. Lower the oven temperature to 170°C (340°F) Gas 4 for the last 10 minutes if the loaf is getting very dark.

27 To check if the loaf is baked, tap it on the bottom. If you hear a hollow sound, it is ready. If not, return it to the oven briefly.

28 Once baked through, allow the loaf to cool on a wire rack.

Sourdough challah

Challah is a Jewish bread eaten on the Sabbath and on holidays. There are two different traditional challah shapes – a snail-shaped one, eaten around New Year to celebrate the circle of life, and a plaited version. It can be eaten with either sweet or savoury food.

TIME PLANNER

Making the pre-ferment **4 hours**

Making the dough **50 minutes**

Letting the dough rise **8 hours–overnight**

Knocking back and shaping the dough **10 minutes**

Final proofing **8 hours**

Baking **35–50 minutes**

Cooling **30 minutes**

INGREDIENTS

390 g/3 cups white strong/bread flour, plus extra for dusting

20 g/4 teaspoons caster/superfine sugar

8 g/1½ teaspoons salt

50 g/50 ml/5 tablespoons sunflower oil

20 g/4 teaspoons warm water (30–37°C/86–99°F)

2 eggs, lightly beaten

egg wash, made from 1 lightly beaten egg mixed with a pinch of salt

poppy seeds or sesame seeds, for topping

For the pre-ferment

130 g/1 cup white strong/bread flour

10 g/2 teaspoons caster/superfine sugar

30 g/1 oz. sourdough starter (see pages 16–17)

130 g/130 ml/½ cup warm water (30–37°C/86–99°F)

EQUIPMENT

1 x 800-g/1¾-lbs. loaf pan

1 baking sheet lined with baking parchment

Makes 1 x 800-g/1¾-lbs. loaf

1 Start by making the pre-ferment. First, add the flour and the sugar to a small mixing bowl and set aside. In a large mixing bowl, dissolve or break up the sourdough starter in the warm water. Add the set-aside flour and sugar mixture and mix together to form a paste consistency. Scrape round the edges and cover with the upturned small mixing bowl. Leave to ferment in a warm place for 4 hours.

2 After 4 hours, the pre-ferment should be bubbling **(A)**. If not, leave to ferment for a further hour until it is bubbling.

3 In a small mixing bowl, mix the flour, sugar and salt together and set aside. This is the dry mixture.

4 In another small mixing bowl, add the oil and water and set aside.

5 Add the lightly beaten egg to the pre-ferment **(B)**. Add the dry mixture, then the oil and water mixture and mix until it comes together. **(C) (D)**

6 At this point, the dough should be slightly sticky but stiff. Cover the mixture with a small mixing bowl.

7 Leave to stand for 10 minutes.

8 Knead the mixture 10 times. Start by squashing the dough with your knuckles and fingers to flatten out any lumps. It should now look pancake-shaped.

9 Lift a portion of the dough up from the side and fold it into the middle and press with your knuckles.

10 Turn the bowl 90° clockwise, lift another portion of the dough up from the side and fold it into the middle and press with your knuckles.

11 Repeat steps 9–10 another 8 times (10 folds in total). If the dough starts to resist and starts to tear, apply less pressure as you knead. Also, if you can only knead it 8 times and it starts to resist, making it difficult to knead, stop.

12 Turn the ball of dough over in the bowl and make a finger mark in the dough (to indicate the first knead).

13 Cover with the small mixing bowl and leave the dough to rest for 10 minutes.

14 Repeat steps 9–13 another 3 times, making sure the mixture is covered between kneads and remembering to mark the dough to indicate the number of kneads done. **(E)**

15 Cover and leave the dough to rise for 4 hours in a warm place (see page 25) **(F)**. Gently punch down to de-gas the dough.

16 Remove the dough and place on a lightly floured work surface. Roll the dough to create one long sausage-shape that tapers slightly at both ends.

17 Roll one end of the sausage inwards to create a spiral snail-shell shape **(G)** and place the loaf on a tray lined with baking parchment.

18 Cover and let the challah rise overnight in a cool place (not in the fridge, though). **(H)**

19 Use a pastry brush to paint the top with egg wash. Sprinkle poppy seeds or sesame seeds on the top. **(I)**

20 Preheat the oven to 250°C (500°F) Gas 9. Place a deep roasting tray at the bottom of the oven.

21 Transfer the loaf to the prepared baking sheet and into the preheated oven. Pour a cup of water into the hot roasting tray. Lower the temperature to 200°C (400°F) Gas 6.

22 Bake for 35–50 minutes until golden brown.

23 Check the loaf is baked by tapping it on the bottom. If you hear a hollow sound, it is ready. If not, return it to the oven briefly.

24 Remove the loaf from the baking sheet and allow to cool on a wire rack.

Variation: To make a plaited/braided challah, follow steps 1–15, then, using a light sprinkling of flour, divide the dough into 6 equal pieces. Roll out the dough into small sausage shapes and then plait/braid all 6 pieces, using the technique shown on page 142. Once plaited, place on a baking sheet lined with baking parchment or into a greased loaf pan and follow steps 18–24.

Chocolate and peanut butter sourdough panettone

This decadent treat is a Christmas crowd-pleaser. It is somewhere between a cake and a bread and is really brought to life with the addition of peanut butter. It does takes two days to make, but it's really worth it. Traditionally, a panettone is hung upside down after baking to aerate the dough, elongate it and stop it falling in on itself. You will need a paper panettone case, a piping bag and two wooden skewers for this recipe.

TIME PLANNER (1ST DOUGH)

Making the dough **50 minutes**

Letting the dough rise **8 hours**

TIME PLANNER (2ND DOUGH)

Making the final dough **60 minutes**

Making the glaze **10 minutes**

Letting the dough rest **30 minutes**

Shaping the dough **10 minutes**

Final proofing **8–16 hours**

Baking **35–45 minutes**

Cooling **30–60 minutes**

Hanging upside down **1 hour**

INGREDIENTS (1ST DOUGH)

200 g/1½ cups strong/bread flour

50 g/¼ cup soft brown sugar

40 g/⅓ stick butter, softened

20 g/4 teaspoons peanut butter

30 g/1 oz. sourdough starter (see pages 16–17)

100 g/100 ml/7 tablespoons warm water (30–37°C/86–99°F)

INGREDIENTS (2ND DOUGH)

30 g/2 tablespoons butter, soft

20 g/4 teaspoons peanut butter

70 g/2½ oz. milk chocolate

20 g/4 teaspoons white strong/bread flour

10 g/2 teaspoons cocoa powder

50 g/¼ cup soft brown sugar

20 g/4 teaspoons runny honey

2 g/½ teaspoon salt

¼ teaspoon vanilla essence

2 egg yolks

For the glaze

10 g/2 teaspoons ground almonds

30 g/2 tablespoons peanut butter

5 g/1 teaspoon cocoa powder

80 g/scant ½ cup sugar

1 egg white

pearl or nibbed sugar, to decorate

Makes 1 x 13.5 cm/5½ in. panettone

1 Assemble the ingredients to make the first dough **(A)**. In a small mixing bowl, mix the flour and the soft brown sugar together and set aside. This is the dry mixture.

2 In a small mixing bowl, mix the soft butter and peanut butter together using a wooden spoon and set aside. This is the butter mixture.

3 In a large mixing bowl, dissolve or break up the sourdough starter (see pages 16–17) in the warm water **(B)**. Add the dry mixture. Mix until it all comes together and there are no dry bits left on the bottom of the bowl. **(C)**

4 Place the butter mixture on top of the dough. Cover the mixture with a small mixing bowl.

5 Leave to stand for 10 minutes.

6 Knead the mixture. Start by squashing the butter mixture into the dough with your knuckles and fingers to incorporate it into the dough. It should now look pancake-shaped.

7 Lift a portion of the dough up from the side and fold into the middle and press with your knuckles. The mixture will get stickier as you work the butter mixture into the dough.

8 Turn the bowl 90° clockwise and lift another portion of the dough up from the side and fold it into the middle and press with your knuckles.

9 Repeat steps 7–8 another 8 times (10 folds in total).

10 Turn the ball of dough over in the bowl and make a finger mark in the dough to indicate the first knead. **(D)**

11 Cover with a small mixing bowl and leave to rest for 10 minutes.

12 Repeat steps 7–11 another 3 times, remembering to mark the dough to indicate the number of kneads done. You are looking for a smooth, elastic dough with the butter mixture fully incorporated into the dough. If you think the dough is not kneaded enough, repeat steps 7–9 another time.

13 Cover and leave the dough to rise for 8 hours in a warm place. **(E)**

14 To make the second dough, in a small mixing bowl, mix the soft butter and peanut butter together using a wooden spoon and set aside. This is the butter mixture.

15 In another small mixing bowl, add the flour and the cocoa powder and set aside.

16 In a third small mixing bowl, whisk the soft brown sugar, honey, salt, vanilla essence and the egg yolks together thoroughly. Add the flour and cocoa powder mixture and mix to a paste consistency. This is the wet mixture.

17 After 8 hours, remove the small mixing bowl that is covering the 1st dough. Add the wet mixture.

18 Knead the mixture. Start by squashing the dough with your knuckles and fingers to incorporate it into the dough. It should now look pancake-shaped and be quite sticky.

19 Lift a portion of the dough up from the side, fold into the middle and press with your knuckles. The mixture will get stickier as you work the wet mixture into the dough.

20 Turn the bowl 90° clockwise and lift another portion of the dough up from the side and fold into the middle and press with your knuckles.

21 Repeat steps 19–20 another 8 times (10 folds in total).

22 Turn the ball of dough over in the bowl and make a finger mark in the dough (to indicate the first knead).

23 Cover with a small mixing bowl and leave to rest for 10 minutes. **(F)**

24 Repeat steps 19–20 twice more, making sure the mixture is covered between kneads and remembering to mark the dough to indicate the number of kneads done.

25 Place the set-aside butter mixture on top. **(G)**

26 Cover and leave to rest for 10 minutes.

27 Repeat steps 19–20 twice more. **(H)**

28 At this stage the butter mixture should be fully incorporated into the dough. If it isn't, knead it another time.

29 Chop the milk chocolate and incorporate it into the dough, repeating steps 19–20. **(I) (J)**

30 Cover and allow the dough to rest for 30 minutes.

31 Place the dough on a lightly oiled work surface. Fold the dough and let rest for a further 30 minutes. **(K)**

32 Shape the dough into a ball (see pages 24–25) and place in the panettone case. Transfer to a baking sheet. **(L)**

33 Cover and leave to proof in a warm place for about 8–16 hours until the dough has tripled in volume and reached the top of the panettone case.

34 Meanwhile, make the glaze by whisking all the ingredients together until smooth. Fill a piping bag with the glaze mixture.

35 After the dough has been proofing for 1 hour, pipe the glaze onto the top of the panettone **(M)**. Re-cover.

36 Preheat the oven to 250°C (500°F) Gas 9.

37 Just before baking, sprinkle some pearl or nibbed sugar on the surface of the fully proofed panettone **(N)**. If the pearl or nibbed sugar does not stick to the glaze, lightly paint the top with water, then sprinkle the pearl or nibbed sugar on the top.

38 Place the panettone on the baking sheet in the preheated oven and lower the oven temperature to 180°C (360°F) Gas 5.

39 Bake the panettone for 35–45 minutes. **(O)**

40 Check if the panettone is baked by tapping it on the bottom. If you can hear a hollow sound, it is ready. If you are not sure, return it to the oven for a further 10 minutes.

41 Remove from the oven. Push the wooden skewers through the panettone case at the bottom of the panettone, making a cross, and hang upside-down over a pot to cool **(P)**.

M　　　　　N　　　　　O　　　　　P

Cranberry and ginger sourdough stollen

Christmas, for me, wouldn't be the same without making stollen and this version, with cranberry, ginger and a marzipan centre, is especially good. Once baked, don't be shy to glaze it with butter – it is Christmas, after all! Coat with vanilla sugar and a little icing/confectioners' sugar.

INGREDIENTS

260 g/2 cups white strong/bread flour, plus extra for dusting

100 g/¾ cup dried cranberries

40 g/2½ tablespoons crystallized ginger, chopped into cranberry-sized pieces

200 g/1½ cups good-quality marzipan (or follow step 5 to make a home-made version)

1 teaspoon ground ginger

100 g/1 stick minus 1 tablespoon butter, softened

40 g/2½ tablespoons demerara/turbinado sugar

½ teaspoon ground cardamom

½ teaspoon vanilla essence

zest of ½ lemon

5 g/½ teaspoon salt

1 egg

80 g/80 ml/⅓ cup warm milk (30–37°C/86–99°F)

150 g/1¼ sticks butter, melted, for glazing

vanilla sugar, for topping

For the pre-ferment

40 g/1½ oz. sourdough starter (see pages 16–17)

40 g/40 ml/2½ tablespoons warm milk (30–37°C/86–99°F)

40 g/⅓ cup white strong/bread flour

Makes 1 large stollen or 2 small stollen

1 To make the pre-ferment, in a large mixing bowl, dissolve or break up the sourdough starter in the warm milk **(A) (B)**, then add the flour and mix into a paste. Scrape the mixture together into a little mound and cover with a small mixing bowl. Leave in a warm place to proof for 4 hours until the pre-ferment starts to bubble.

2 While the pre-ferment rises, in a small mixing bowl, add the flour and set aside. This is the dry mixture.

3 In another small mixing bowl, mix the dried cranberries and the crystallized ginger and set aside. This is the fruit mixture.

4 In a third small mixing bowl, mix the marzipan with the ground ginger and shape into a ball. Cover with a shower cap so it does not dry out. Alternatively, make home-made marzipan by mixing 120 g/1¼ cups ground almonds, 60 g/4 tablespoons caster/superfine sugar, 1 teaspoon ground ginger and 2 tablespoons water together and shape into a ball.

5 In another large mixing bowl, add the soft butter, demerara sugar, cardamom, vanilla essence, lemon zest and salt **(C)**.

Beat using a balloon whisk or wooden spoon until soft.

6 Whisk the egg into the soft butter mixture **(D)**. If the mixture separates and curdles, mix in about 2 tablespoons of the dry mixture to bind the mixture together.

7 After 4 hours, the pre-ferment should be bubbling. If not, leave to ferment for another hour until it is bubbling.

8 Uncover the bubbling pre-ferment and mix in the warm milk and the dry mixture **(E)**. Place the butter mixture on top **(F)**. Mix with your hands until it comes together **(G)**. The dough should be slightly sticky.

9 Cover the mixture with a small upturned mixing bowl and leave to stand for 10 minutes.

10 Knead the mixture. Start by squashing the dough with your knuckles and fingers to flatten out lumps. It should now look pancake-shaped.

11 Lift a portion of the dough up from the side, fold it into the middle and press it with your knuckles.

A   B   C   D

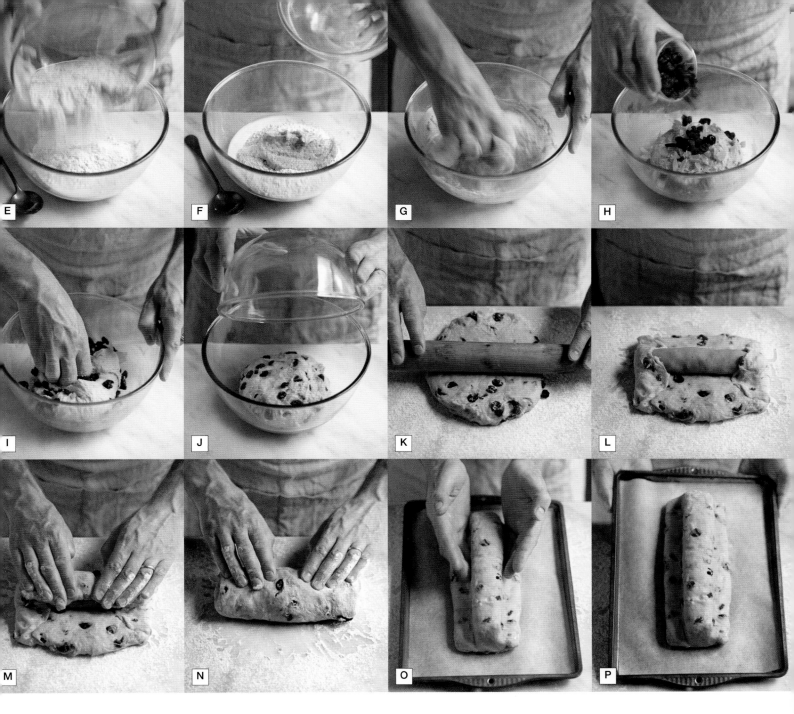

12 Turn the bowl 90° clockwise and lift another portion of the dough up from the side and fold into the middle and press with your knuckles.

13 Repeat steps 11–12 another 8 times (10 folds in total).

14 Turn the ball of dough over in the bowl and, make a finger mark in the dough (to indicate the first knead).

15 Cover with a small mixing bowl and let rest for 10 minutes.

16 Repeat steps 11–15 one more time.

17 Add the fruit mixture (H) and repeat steps 12–16 twice more, making sure the mixture is covered between kneads and remembering to mark the dough to indicate the number of kneads you have done. All the fruit should now be evenly distributed into the dough. (I)

18 Cover and leave the dough to rise in a warm place for 1 hour. **(J)**

19 After 1 hour, remove the dough from the bowl, and, using a light sprinkling of flour, shape into a ball.

20 First, flatten the dough slightly with your palm. Then, take a corner of the dough and fold it right over to the opposite side, then turn the dough 90° clockwise.

21 Repeat the previous step 4–5 more times until the dough is a roundish shape. Then turn the dough over and tuck in the underneath of the dough with your fingers as you rotate the dough clockwise until you've formed a rounded ball. Leave to rest for 10 minutes.

22 While the dough is resting, remove the marzipan from the bowl and shape into a long sausage shape, about 20 cm/ 8 inches long.

23 After the dough has rested for 10 minutes, shape it into a stollen shape. Do this by first turning the ball over, then flattening it into an oval shape, and then rolling it out about 2 cm/¾ inch thick, still keeping its oval shape **(K)**. Place the marzipan sausage in the centre, making sure that there is room to fold the sides of the dough over the marzipan.

24 Fold the sides inwards and over the marzipan so it becomes a rectangular shape with the marzipan in the middle **(L)**. Using your hands or a rolling pin, roll the top and bottom part of the dough, making sure the marzipan is wedged between the sides that are folded in. **(M)**

25 Fold the top part over the marzipan, then the bottom part over the top. **(N)**

26 Place the stollen on the prepared baking sheet seam-side down.

27 Using the blade of your hand, press the dough in the middle to form a stollen shape (a raised ridge), making sure no marzipan comes through. **(O) (P)**

28 Cover and allow to proof in a warm place for 2–6 hours or until the dough has nearly doubled in volume. **(Q)**

29 Preheat the oven to 220°C (425°F) Gas 7. Place a deep roasting tray at the bottom of the oven.

30 Place the baking sheet in the oven and pour a cup of water into the hot roasting tray to form steam. Lower the temperature to 180°C (350°F) Gas 4.

31 Bake for 35–40 minutes until golden brown.

32 Check that it is baked by tapping on the bottom. If you hear a hollow sound, it is ready. If you are not sure, return it to the oven for a further 10 minutes.

33 Place on a wire rack to cool slightly.

34 Remove any dark cranberries that caught while baking with a sharp knife, taking care not to damage the stollen.

35 Use a pastry brush to paint the stollen with hot melted butter 3 times on the top **(R)**, then 3 times on the bottom **(S)**. Take care not to damage the stolen and allow the butter to sink into the stollen before painting it again.

36 Once the final coating of butter has set, roll the stollen in vanilla sugar and sprinkle some more on top **(T)**. Finish by dusting with icing/confectioners' sugar and serve.

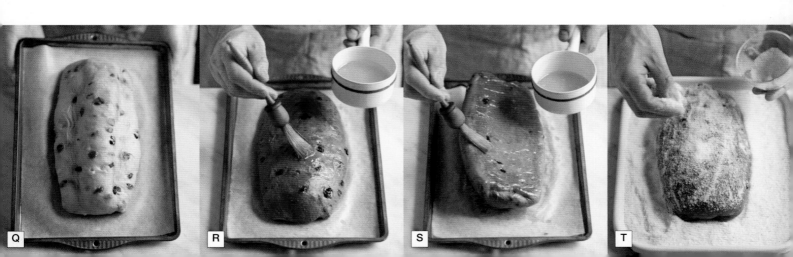

Q · R · S · T

Suppliers and stockists

UK

Fresh yeast can be bought from bakeries and most supermarkets with in-store bakeries.

Shipton Mill
Long Newnton
Tetbury
Gloucestershire GL8 8RP
Tel: +44 (0)1666 505050
www.shipton-mill.com
For many, many types of organic flour, milled on site, available to buy online in small or large quantities. It also stocks fresh yeast, organic yeast and proofing/dough-rising baskets. Its website is also a good reference for the mechanics of flour and grains.

Doves Farm
Salisbury Road
Hungerford
Berkshire RG17 0RF
Tel: +44 (0)1488 684880
www.dovesfarm.co.uk
Like Shipton Mill, Doves Farm supplies many, many types of organic flour, milled on site and available to buy online in small or large quantities, as well as all sorts of other organic products. It stocks a large range of proofing/dough-rising baskets in all sizes and shapes.

www.brotformen.de
Tel: +49 (0)34 364 522 87
German supplier of proofing/dough-rising baskets in all manner of shapes and sizes.

BakeryBits
1 Orchard Units, Duchy Road
Honiton
Devon EX14 1YD
Tel: +44 (0)1404 565656
www.bakerybits.co.uk
Online supplier of every kind of tool, utensil and equipment needed to bake bread.

Lakeland
Tel: +44 (0)1539 488100
www.lakeland.co.uk
Stockists of bakeware and cookware, with branches around the UK, as well as an excellent website.

Divertimenti
Tel: +44 (0)330 333 0351
www.divertimenti.co.uk
Cookware stockist, with branches in London and Cambridge, as well as an online store.

Nisbets
Tel: +44 (0)845 140 5555
www.nisbets.co.uk
Enormous range of catering equipment to buy online, including loaf pans and more, plus branches in London and Bristol.

Traditional Cornmillers Guild
www.tcmg.org.uk
For details of individual mills around the UK.

US

King Arthur Flour
Tel: +1 800 827 6836
www.kingarthurflour.com
America's oldest – and one of the best – flour company. Flours are unbleached and never bromated. Its great selection of flours includes 9-grain flour blend, malted wheat flakes, Irish-style wholemeal/wholewheat flour, French-style flour for baguettes, European-style artisan bread flour, as well as sugar, yeast in bulk, sourdough starters, baking pans, proofing/dough-rising baskets, bread/pizza peels and other bakeware and equipment.

Bob's Red Mill
Tel: +1 800 349 2173
www.bobsredmill.com
Online supplier of traditional and gluten-free flours, plus grains and seeds.

Hodgson Mill
Tel: +1 800 525 0177
www.hodgsonmill.com
Suppliers of all-natural, whole grains and stoneground products.

Breadtopia
Tel: +1 800 469 7989
www.breadtopia.com
From dough scrapers to proofing/dough-rising baskets and sourdough starters, this Iowa-based company has every gadget and pan an artisan bread baker could ever want.

La Cuisine – The Cook's Resource
Tel: +1 800 521 1176
www.lacuisineus.com
Fine bakeware including oval and round proofing/dough-rising baskets, loaf pans in every size and bread/pizza peels.

Crate & Barrel
Tel: +1 630 369 4464
www.crateandbarrel.com
Good stockist of bakeware online and in stores throughout the country.

Sur la table
Tel: +1 800 243 0852
www.surlatable.com
Good stockist of bakeware online and in stores throughout the country.

Williams-Sonoma
Tel: +1 877 812 6235
www.williams-sonoma.com
Good stockist of bakeware online and in stores throughout the country.

www.sigridhovmand.dk
Danish potter and maker of the Bread Dome (Dutch oven) pictured on pages 9, 26 and 35. This unglazed stoneware dome helps achieve a crisp crust and retain the bread's moisture and taste. It is available in 3 sizes.

Index

Acknowledgements

I would like to thank the following people for their help with this book:

My wife Lisa and son Noah, my biggest supporters, for their enthusiasm and patience through the whole project.

Steve Painter for his patience, attention to detail and great talent in taking pictures that tell the story of *How To Make Sourdough*.

Thanks to Jethro Marriage from Doves Farm, John Lister and Tom Russell from Shipton Mill, Hannah Marriage from Marriages and Michael Stoats from Cann Mills for sponsoring the flour used in the book and lots of bits of equipment, Patrick Thornberry and Vanessa Kimbell from BakeryBits and Eric and Denyce Rusch from Breadtopia. To Dave Redding for making the wooden peels and Leigh Dyer for the metal peels.

Thanks to Clare Monk from the Welbeck Brewery for all the fresh beer barm and malt, and also Tony Champion from the Filo Brewery and Pete Mason at Hastings Brewery for the barm used in the book.

Thanks to The School of Artisan Food, where I teach, for lending me some of the equipment used in the book as props. To Maria Mayerhofer and Benazir Amein (Benny) from Baking With Maria for all their positive feedback as the book progressed.

Also to David Carter for his words of wisdom and helping with some of the research and text for the book and Pete Smith for the milk kefir grains.

Massive thanks to Tess Eaton and Andrew Swan for letting me bake at the Crown Pub in Hastings, together with all the customers who tasted the bread.

Nathan Joyce for his patience and understanding in editing the book and his great diplomacy.

Lastly, to everyone that had a little say in the book, tasting the breads or testing the recipes, a big thank you to all of you.